Slayers

VOL. 4: THE BATTLE OF SAILLUNE

WRITTEN BY
HAJIME KANZAKA

ILLUST
RUI A

D1160792

TOKYOPOP®

HAMBURG // LONDON // LOS ANGELES // TOKYO

Slayers Vol. 4: The Battle of Saillune
Written by Hajime Kanzaka
Illustrated by Rui Araizumi

Translation - Jeremiah Bourque
English Adaptation - Jay Antani
Associate Editors - Lianne Sentar and Peter Ahlstrom
Design and Layout - Jose Macasocol, Jr.
Cover Design - Jorge Negrete

Editor - Nicole Monastirsky
Digital Imaging Manager - Chris Buford
Pre-Press Manager - Antonio DePietro
Production Managers - Jennifer Miller and Mutsumi Miyazaki
Art Director - Matt Alford
Managing Editor - Jill Freshney
VP of Production - Ron Klamert
Editor-in-Chief - Mike Kiley
President and C.O.O. - John Parker
Publisher and C.E.O. - Stuart Levy

A  Novel

TOKYOPOP Inc.
5900 Wilshire Blvd. Suite 2000
Los Angeles, CA 90036

E-mail: info@TOKYOPOP.com
Come visit us online at www.TOKYOPOP.com

ISBN: 1-59532-580-8

First TOKYOPOP printing: June 2005
10 9 8 7 6 5 4 3 2 1
Printed in the USA

CONTENTS

1: SURPRISED TO BE INVOLVED (PER USUAL)

It was a clear night, and the air was crisp and bracing. The moon and the stars cast an ethereal glow on the Royal Palace towering before us. In different circumstances, you might've thought the setting was downright romantic. But romance was the furthest thing from my mind. I was with Gourry—not exactly a guy with a knack for romancing a girl. That aside, we were on a mission.

On either side of the enormous closed gates that led to the Palace were twin turrets, each topped with great lanterns that glowed eerily in the night.

"We'll sneak in through here," I whispered to Gourry from behind a tree that hid us from the road.

"You mean we have to stop hiding now?" Gourry's voice trembled in the dark. He was the deadliest swordsman I'd ever met, but he could also be the biggest baby as things got even a mite scary. So it was no surprise that he resisted the idea of venturing out into the open, or that he tried to protest it in completely ineffective whisper-yells.

Oh, and just so we're straight, Gourry and I aren't bandits. We don't make it our profession to go sneaking into mansions and palaces to steal people's valuables.

Though, I admit, I've been tempted now and again.

But looks can be deceiving. Poking around the woods like that, in the cover of night, we made an awfully suspicious pair. If townspeople spotted us and started hollering, "Stop, thief!" and pelting us with rocks, it would've been impossible to explain ourselves. And, if you saw me, you might've been convinced I was a bandit. And a damn sexy one at that!

From head to toe, I was a vision in black. I wore a slim-fitting pair of trousers over a tunic I'd bought somewhere in our travels. The tunic was tight and pinched my armpits and butt, but I still looked ever so fetching in it, if I do say so myself. Girding my waist was a leather belt that showed off my curvy hips. Okay, maybe they aren't so curvy, but a girl can dream, right? Finally, lending that touch of mystique to my ensemble, I wore a mask. If only I could see through those ratty little holes I'd cut into my mask, I might have tripped and stumbled a bit less as we made our way through the woods.

Both Gourry and I wore swords at our sides, only adding to the impression that we were a couple of assassins trying to infiltrate the Royal Palace. But, hey, you're never going to find me on a mission without my weapon, no matter what some naïve passerby might think. It was a difficult game of stealth, but I, Lina Inverse—the greatest sorceress this world has ever seen—was ready for danger!

Plus, what kind of girl do you think I am? I would never take a job where I had to kill and steal from the *good guys*. I got standards, you know.

"We'll sneak in through this way 'cause it's where they'd least expect it," I reasoned with Gourry.

"*That's* your thinking?" he snapped back at me. "Just because they don't expect it doesn't mean they won't be waiting for us with their pointy spears."

"Oh, stop whining," I shot back as I crept out toward the road. Gourry didn't budge from behind the tree. "Let's go!" I whispered to him as loudly as I could and gestured for him to make tracks.

He protested a little more—how funny to see Gourry, the bearer of the Sword of Light, acting like a wiener. When he finally snuck toward me, I rolled my eyes and stealthily led the way.

"This city is in worse shape than I ever imagined," Sylphiel said in a meek voice, sniffling tears away as she gazed into her after-dinner mint tea and pushed aside her long, glossy black hair. She was a little older than me and strikingly beautiful. And, in her sleek priestess' robes, she really did look quite dazzling.

Damn her!

We sat in a hole-in-the-wall restaurant in some tucked-away alley. The grub wasn't bad, but business was slow. It wasn't because of the location, as you might suspect—it seemed business was dead-as-a-doornail on every avenue we'd walked down.

That was a shock. We were in Saillune City, after all, the capitol of the Holy Kingdom of Saillune. It had always thrived with merchants and artisans, a great center of learning, culture, and music. But all that had changed lately. Now, it was in the midst of complete turmoil.

We hadn't come all that way just for sightseeing, though. We were escorting Sylphiel, who wanted to stay with relatives in Saillune City after losing her other family. Gourry and I wanted to keep her away from trouble, and in Saillune, trouble-making was practically a requirement for residency.

"What's this city in such a big mess for, anyway?" Gourry stared blankly into space. My traveling companion was a handsome male specimen and a lethal swordsman if there ever was one, but I sometimes suspected warm bean paste sat where his brain ought to be.

"Um," I managed, trying not to choke on my pork sausage. More than anything, I wanted to bonk him on the forehead with my salad fork, but I resisted. Sylphiel struggled to gulp down her mint tea, while I could feel her eyes narrow.

With both of my hands, I pressed down hard on my temples. It was all I could do to keep my head from bursting with frustration.

"Wait a sec," I said through gritted teeth. "Are you trying to tell me you have no idea why this city is in the state it's in? Haven't you been listening?"

Gourry blinked. "Listening to what?"

"Whaa!" I erupted. "It's all Sylphiel and I have been talking about during our whole trip here! Where have you been?!"

"Do you think I actually waste my time *listening* to everything you say, Lina?" He shook his head and chuckled, clearly proud of his remark.

"Shut your pie hole!" Not the snappiest comeback, but it was all I could muster considering how frazzled Gourry had gotten me. "And don't smile so much—you look like an idiot," I added for affect before sinking back in my chair with a groan.

"Anyway," I said, returning to my plate. "The short version is that there's a major family feud going on here, and this city is ground zero."

"Huh," replied Gourry, biting into a turnip.

"About six months ago," I continued, slowly and clearly for Gourry's sake, "the king fell ill. He's still got his marbles, but he's in no physical shape to get out of bed, much less rule his kingdom. No one knows for sure, though. It's all rumor."

"Hmm," replied Gourry, biting into another turnip. I still wasn't sure he was listening.

"So that started all this talk about who'll take the throne after the king dies. And that's when all this trouble started brewing."

"Huh." And there he went munching on his fifth turnip. That got me worried; not only was Gourry a little slow on the uptake, but turnips cause severe gas.

If he was going to ignore me now and stink up the inn later, I was going to have to get rough with him. I used every last fiber of my patience to keep from jamming that turnip up his nose. I leaned in toward him, since what I had to tell next was best told in secret. I still made sure to breathe through my mouth.

"A bunch of assassins—hired by either the townsfolk or members of the royal house—have begun making attempts to rub out the First Royal Successor. Since the successor's apparently aware of this, he's ferreted himself away from his own palace and is probably curled up in the fetal position somewhere in the city."

Gourry nodded his head solemnly. "The bottom line," I went on, "is that now Saillune City is crawling with all sorts of assassins and conspirators eager to take over the throne." I sat back and took a deep breath. "Got it?"

Gourry stared at me with intent, unblinking eyes, then shook his head. "Not really."

"Ughhh!! I shrieked as I lunged for Gourry's neck. "You brick-headed mushbrain!"

"Hey!" Gourry cried. "Lina, calm down! I'm kidding! I get it!"

Gourry sat back down and sighed. "Hey," he asked. "Um, what's the deal with this First Royal Successor, anyway?"

I braced for the worst and just tried to breathe deeply.

Sylphiel knitted her eyebrows in disbelief.

"It's all right, Sylphiel, let me handle this." I turned back to Gourry and growled, "What are you talking about?! The First Royal Successor is *the first in line to take the throne!*"

"No, it's not that," Gourry answered mildly. "I was just wondering why you're calling him that. Isn't *First Royal Successor* just a fancy way of saying he's the prince?"

Twitch!

"Well, yes," Sylphiel said calmly. Her eyes had that faraway look they often had, like she was daydreaming. "The Prince of Saillune, you could say, is hiding somewhere in this city from royally-appointed assassins. It's rather . . . romantic, isn't it?" She melted into her words with a long sigh.

"Jeez!" I was surrounded! A dim-witted swordsman on one side, and a sappy schoolgirl on the other. Can't a certifiably sane sorceress catch a break in this world?!

As I leaned back, the legs of my chair slid out from under me, and I went tumbling to the floor. I slumped there, festooned with salad leaves, and fumed. Life can be cruel sometimes, can't it?

"Hey, Lina!" said Gourry, craning over the table to have a look at me. "What's wrong?!"

"Did something happen?" Sylphiel blinked.

I picked a piece of shrimp off my tunic and munched on it. *Not bad.*

"It's nothing," I grunted, chewing.

Then, as calmly as I could, I picked myself up off the floor, straightened out my chair and, with a deep breath, sat back down. All I wanted was to finish my meal in peace.

I decided not to tell Sylphiel or Gourry that I'd actually met the First Royal Successor before. It had been awhile back, but he'd certainly left a lasting impression, and not necessarily a flattering one. But I wasn't about to burst Sylphiel's bubble—I figured I'd let her have her fantasies for the time being.

"Anyway, Sylphiel," I said after a minute. "Just to be on the safe side, you told your relatives you were on your way here, didn't you? So they know we're coming?"

"I did," Sylphiel replied. "I sent a message to them back in Cannon City. They should've gotten it by now."

This was puzzling. We'd been in the restaurant all evening, but none of her relatives had shown up to meet us. "I wonder what's holding them up?" I asked. "Some priestly duties or something? What do you think?"

Sylphiel took a sip of her tea. "I suppose that's it." I sensed some wariness in her tone, and her face seemed to have darkened. She thought for a moment, then added, "To be honest, what I need is a job. I need to stand on my own two feet; my parents' death convinced me of that." She shook her head and stared at her tea. "But look at the mess this city is in. I'd be lucky to find a job sweeping the street."

"Look," I told her sternly. "You can find a job once things settle down. Right now, we've got bigger fish to fry."

I love food metaphors. They're yummy.

Sylphiel nodded her head but kept her eyes lowered. I might not have cheered her up, but at least Gourry was keeping quiet. We gathered our things a few minutes later and ventured out into the darkening city.

"Over there!" Sylphiel shouted excitedly. "The house with the brown tiled roof." We stood on a quiet street, high above the city. The house she pointed to was just outside the Royal Palace in a district full of monuments and mansions.

About time, I thought, keeping it in my head to be polite. And before you ask your next question, yes, I *can* be polite.

It wasn't just that Sylphiel's family's place was about three times as far as I'd expected it to be. There was something very unsettling about walking through the near-deserted Saillune City, particularly at night. There are few things more depressing than a thriving city on the skids—

I mean, the lack of fried meat products being sold on the street was almost enough to make a grown sorceress cry.

Before long, we were in front of the high walls that fortified the Royal Palace and Sylphiel's home-to-be. It wasn't very large—a mansion but on the small side, you might say— but it was sturdily built and beautiful. Just like me.

Sylphiel was spellbound by the sight of her family's home. She looked back at us with a peaceful expression. "If it's not too much trouble, would you mind coming in for a minute?" she asked Gourry.

"Uh . . . yeah," he muttered. I couldn't expect him to be any more articulate than that. Then he turned to me with a wary look on his face, scratching his cheek.

"Yeah, Sylphiel," I piped in. "This is as good a time as any to meet your family."

I figured that delivering her to her family would conclude our arrangement: She would be properly deposited in Saillune City and could then settle up with the rest of the cash. It would be a good place to say our farewells and make sure she was squared away in her new surroundings among a bunch of people who, I might add, she barely knew. I like to make sure my clients are safe and happy when my business is finished. I'm like that.

Besides, Sylphiel still needed to explain exactly what had happened to her parents, and I figured it'd be best if Gourry and I were there to help fill in details. Gourry and I stood behind her as she clanged the wolf's head knocker on the door several times. The air was still and silent after that, and we waited.

"Is no one home?" I finally asked.

Sylphiel shrugged her shoulders and slowly reached for the knocker again. But just as she did so, we sensed a presence on the other side of the door. The shuffling of feet and muttering of a voice sounded from inside the house.

The door groaned open just a crack, and a middle-aged man's face appeared behind it. I got the feeling he had aged prematurely: there was life in his eyes, but his face was furrowed, and there were streaks of white running through his chestnut hair. He definitely gave the impression of a man with a lot on his mind.

His eyes settled on Sylphiel and he immediately beamed. "Ah!" he cried. "Sylphiel!" He threw the door open, flinging his arms out to give her a hug.

She ran into his embrace. "It's been a long time, Grandpa Gray," Sylphiel squeaked as she choked back her tears. I have to admit, I was a little veklempt myself.

"Too long," Grandpa Gray replied in his thin, crackly voice. He shook his head and stared at her in disbelief. "My, my, you were but a child the last time I saw you. You've grown quite pretty indeed."

He looked at her, taking in the warmth and joy of the moment, and then realized we were standing out in the open.

"Oh, but this is no place to dilly-dally," he said. As he motioned for her to come inside, his eyes fell on Gourry and me.

He raised a bony trembling hand toward us. "And these people?" he asked. "Who are they?" I couldn't help but sense his suspicion. Frankly, it irritated me—after all, we'd just escorted his dear Sylphiel all the way there, and I'd have appreciated a simple *thank you* instead of a leery eye.

Sylphiel clasped her hands and turned toward us. "This is Miss Lina and Mister Gourry. They saved my life in Sairaag and escorted me all the way here."

"My pleasure," Mr. Gray muttered as he peered at us with his heavy-lidded eyes.

Mr. Gray wasn't exactly the personable type, but times were rough and such that you couldn't trust anybody anymore. I tried to keep that in mind as I took in Mr. Gray's lousy attitude.

"Then I must certainly thank you for your troubles," Mr. Gray offered.

Spare me the civility and gimme my money.

"No need to thank us," I said haltingly. "It was our pleasure."

"They were also involved in what happened in Sairaag," Sylphiel said, stammering a bit. "I thought they could better explain the details to you."

"I see . . ." Mr. Gray nodded with a huff. His eyes kept darting back and forth; he certainly didn't seem reassured, and in fact, he was starting to give me the willies. "Perhaps tomorrow we could arrange some sort of—"

"Grandfather!" Sylphiel snapped, raising her eyebrows sternly. I'd never seen that side of her, and I gotta say I was impressed.

"We don't mind at all," I said with a wave of my arms. "We just wanted to say hello and see Sylphiel off. We'll take our leave and leave you be."

I noticed a sudden change wash over Mr. Gray. "Ah, yes," he mumbled. He shuffled his feet and stammered, searching for a way to apologize. "It's just that at the moment, the place is a bit . . . uh . . . unsightly. Yes! There's a mess everywhere. Let me go in and tidy up a bit before I welcome you in." He twittered strangely and backed away.

What's up with him? Who's he kidding with all that yammering and shuffling?

Having squeaked out his little explanation, Mr. Gray slammed his door shut. From outside, we could hear rustling and puttering as he shoved things here and there.

"I wonder what's come over Grandfather?" Sylphiel thought aloud. She frowned and leaned up against a pillar, clearly upset. I couldn't help but be a bit weirded out myself. As for Gourry, I wasn't sure he was taking any of this in; he just stood in the walkway, sniffing and chewing his fingernails.

We waited like that for what seemed like hours until Mr. Gray, with groomed hair and a fresh caftan, opened the door again and beckoned us inside. I caught a whiff of perfumes and bath oils as we entered the house and it reminded me that I needed a shower myself. Being a fortune-seeking adventurer can be hot, dirty work.

"I'm sorry to have kept you waiting," Mr. Gray said. "Make yourselves comfortable." He smiled, but I could tell he was trying awfully hard to be friendly.

Hey, buddy, don't go through the trouble of being nice on my account. I'm used to jerks in this business.

Gourry and I glanced at each other and shrugged as we followed Sylphiel into the house.

"Here you go," said a woman who was probably Mr. Gray's wife, as she skipped in carrying a tea tray. "It's not much to offer on such notice."

"Thank you very much," I muttered as I poured myself a cup of tea and looked over at Mr. Gray. That weirdo still had a fake smile plastered on his face. If he wasn't our client's grandfather, I swear I would've slapped the smile off right then and there.

"How's Toran?" Sylphiel asked.

Mr. Gray looked vacantly at Sylphiel. "My son? He married a short time back. He opened a magic healing shop not far from here and we see him from time to time." He cleared his throat and shifted in his chair. "Anyway," he added, perking considerably, "what happened back in Sairaag?"

Whoah, he sure dropped that *subject like a hot potato. Hmm . . . hot potatoes, not a bad idea.*

Sylphiel, was who perched like a bird in her chair, blurted, "I think Miss Lina can explain everything better than I can."

"Ugh," I groaned. If I had to explain everything, going back to when Gourry and I first met, I'd be running at the mouth all evening and into the night. And, after days of arduous travel, I just didn't have it in me.

"I guess," I began. "Er . . . so first, there was Gourry and—"

"You! You're that sorceress, aren't you?!" blared a voice from the doorway.

I was relieved for the distraction, but not so relieved by what had distracted me. At the half-open door that led to the hallway stood a funny-looking man.

He was a stocky, bearded, chunky-looking fellow, not unlike a dwarf. In fact, he looked exactly like a dwarf—a dwarf that had been stretched out like dough with a rolling pin. Not a pretty sight. He looked about forty years old and could pass for a bandit chieftain if you smeared him with dirt, dressed him in chain mail, and broke a few more of his crooked teeth.

I knew that nasty face all too well.

"You know this little girl?" Mr. Gray asked, rather bewildered.

Little girl? It's bad enough hearing that from Gourry, but a total stranger?!

Sylphiel's and Mr. Gray's eyeballs ping-ponged between the doorway-man and me, while Gourry just sat there, calmly nibbling on finger food and sipping tea.

The man chuckled heartily. "Yes, I do know her," he said confidently. "You can put your mind at rest, Mr. Gray. She's someone we can trust."

Mr. Gray turned back to me and sighed as if a boulder had been lifted from his shoulders.

"Um, Grandfather. . . who is that strange man?" Sylphiel asked nervously.

"This is, uh . . ." He sat up and said in a low, secretive tone, "I must not say it so loudly."

He cast a look at the strange man, then back at his granddaughter. "This . . . is Master Philionel El Di Saillune. The First Royal Successor of the Holy Kingdom of Saillune."

Now it was out.

After a short pause, Sylphiel squeaked an "Excuse me?" in a faint, broken voice. Little by little, she leaned in toward me.

"The P-P-*Prince?*" she whispered.

I turned to her and nodded gravely.

Sorry you had to find out like this, kid. The truth hurts, don't it?

"Oh . . ." she moaned weakly. Then, sinking in her chair like a bag of dirt, she passed out.

★★★

After all the introductions, I began filling our guests in on the Sairaag episode. Just then, Mr. Gray's wife appeared. She'd just been checking in on our fainting patient who was recuperating in her bed upstairs.

"Ah! Maria, how is Sylphiel doing?" Mr. Gray asked.

Maria shook her head and took a seat, a tiny smile on her lips.

"She's sleeping peacefully," she reported. "She was making terrible moaning sounds earlier, but now she's nodded off, the poor thing."

"I bet she's just tuckered out from her journey. Now that she's safe and sound, she finally feels safe to rest, you know?" I laughed as pleasantly as I could, wondering if I was at all convincing.

"Perhaps so," said Mr. Gray in a weary tone and nodding his head.

Of course, I didn't want to let on as to why Sylphiel had really passed out.

The shock had been too great, no doubt. Here she was imagining that the Prince of Saillune was this dreamy hunk of man only to find out that her dream prince was really a short, wart-nosed, middle-aged ogre. It's too great a shock for almost anyone to bear, let alone a boy-crazy female of mating age. I can't say I didn't see it coming.

As for the ogre-prince, I'd run into him awhile back when he was on a secret mission of his own. So I had a bit of a heads-up on the situation.

Okay, I admit I was a little bummed out by this so-called prince. But it wasn't just his looks—his personality bothered me to no end. He was so aggravating, I couldn't think straight.

Phil finally sat up, his palms joined. "Well, then," he said. "I think it's my turn to explain matters." He bowed his head slowly and deeply as if he were trying to collect his thoughts.

He said there *had* been an assassination attempt on his royal life, but by using his skills of persuasion he'd been able to protect himself. Unfortunately, right after that, his people began to get knocked off like dominoes. Greatly disturbed by this turn of events, Phil had fled the Royal Palace in the hopes of baiting the assassins away from his courtiers and back to him. Since then, Phil had been in hiding in Mr. Gray's home—a move that, so far, had been successful. His enemies hadn't rooted him out and no one else in the royal court had been assassinated.

So that was why Mr. Gray had been nervous letting Gourry and me into his home. To him, we may as well have been assassins, and Mr. Gray wasn't about to do something reckless and endanger his prince's life.

Phil stood up and bowed again. "I believe I owe you an apology for all the trouble I caused you, Gray."

"Excellency," replied Mr. Gray, falling down on one knee, "it is my honor. You need not waste such words on me."

Phil suddenly swung himself in our direction. "Now then, Miss Lina and Mr. Gourry," he announced. "There's one thing I would ask of you, if possible."

The two of us looked at each other.

Great—here it comes.

We couldn't exactly dash out of there. As much as Phil disgusted me, you can't turn down a request made by a bona fide prince.

Dammit! Who wrote that rule? Let me at him!

"We're just humble travelers," I stammered, stealing a glance at Gourry, whose eyes looked like they were about to pop out of his head. "We can't offer to do much, but we'd be honored to hear your request."

"As I mentioned before, I departed from the Royal Palace and have been in hiding for quite some time. My courtiers may have grown fearful for my safety, and I merely want to send them word that I'm alive and well. Any doubt to the contrary could lead to disaster; to avert that, I wish them to know I'm all right."

Phil gestured toward Mr. Gray. "Gray here attends to his duties at the Temple of the Royal Palace once every five days, but I feel it would be too dangerous for a citizen of his standing to attempt this task." He spun on his heels and leaned toward me. "So it falls to you, Miss Lina and Mr. Gourry."

"I s-s-see," I managed and folded my arms. From where I stood, I could smell the prince's breath. Unfortunately for me, he'd had liver and onions for lunch.

It was obvious, given how dangerous the situation was, that we couldn't just waltz through the front door of the Royal Palace to deliver the prince's message. Could we perhaps get in contact with someone from the palace while he or she was out and about?

Drat! That wouldn't work either. It was way too dangerous for any member of the royalty to go traipsing around town unprotected. If they had to leave the palace, which was rare nowadays, it would only be in the company of soldiers.

That left us with one option: sneaking in.

I had to admit; the idea got my juices flowing. I was in the mood for a little adventure.

"There are two people to whom I would entrust my message," Phil said. "Conveying it to either of them will be sufficient. Neither of them must risk the danger of outside exposure, so to fulfill the task, you will need to infiltrate the Royal Palace. I dare say it's dangerous work."

No! Really?

"But—" A voice broke in. It was Gourry's; I couldn't believe he was actually listening, much less speaking up. "Do you have any clue who the leader of these assassins might be?"

Huh, did Mr. Bean paste just ask an intelligent question?

Of course, if Phil knew the name of their leader, there would be no reason for him to go through all this trouble just to deliver a message. He'd just have to take the baddies out with the rest of the garbage, and his troubles would be over.

Phil stood for a while stroking his chin whiskers with his stubby fingers before grunting, "There *is* somebody I suspect. Indeed, I can't imagine it being anyone else." He pounded a fist into his palm before adding, "The problem is I lack definite proof."

"Well," I shrugged, "if you're *almost* sure who it is, why don't Gourry and I sneak into the palace, find your man, and give him the smackdown of his life?" I twirled my sword in my hands. It had been too long since my last smackdown.

Phil chuckled and twiddled his fingers. He appeared to actually consider my suggestion for a moment before he narrowed his eyes and shot me a hard look.

"You don't understand," he said sternly. "My appearance may be deceiving, but I'm a pacifist. I would never resort to violence before exhausting any and all peaceful means of resolving conflict." Phil flung his stocky arms behind his back and began pacing the room.

"Besides," he went on, "I need incontrovertible proof that he is indeed the mastermind, including accounts from eyewitnesses I could trust, before I mete out any punishment upon him."

Ugh . . . think things through? B-o-r-i-n-g.

I live for action, you see. If you tell me such-and-such is the bad guy, then get out of my way—I'm hunting that sucker down and beating him within an inch of his life. But Phil obviously liked to play by the rules and he was already stretching my patience pretty thin as it was.

Phil whipped around and faced us. For a stubby old guy, he was awfully fleet-footed. "Now, getting back to delivering my message. First, I'd like to know if you agree to the task before I tell you whom to deliver it to. There's certainly no pressure; you may refuse if you wish and be happily on your way." He kept looking from me to Gourry with one of those grim, this-is-no-joke kind of looks.

All right, all right. We'll play the game your way. Sheesh.

I nodded in agreement and smiled as innocently as I could.

"We're in this already," I said. "Helping Sylphiel get her here safely was our job. But after seeing this city in the mess it's in, it's obvious it was only a *part* of the job. Let's finish it."

"My apologies," Phil replied, bowing deeply. He even seemed a little teary-eyed. "I judged you both rather hastily."

I admit, Phil seemed like a standup guy. When he felt badly about something, he apologized with the modesty of one of his own subjects. He was a class act in that regard.

"Very well," he went on. "I need my message delivered to two people: Clawfell, my closest aide, and Amelia."

"Amelia?" I repeated. "That's a weird name for a guy."

Phil smiled at my remark, and something glinted in his beady dark eyes.

"She's a woman, actually." He beamed. "Amelia is my daughter."

"Daughter?!" Gourry and I blurted. I had to catch my breath, I was so caught off guard.

Phil having a daughter would mean that—how to put this mildly?—he had *mated* with someone. That was not only a frightening thought, it downright turned my stomach.

And theoretically this daughter would *look* like Phil. *Yikes!*

My facial tics must've been less than subtle, because I noticed Mr. Gray glaring at me severely. "She's *quite* pretty," he snapped, hurling the words like darts. He leaned back in his chair and added, "She looks so much like her mother."

Ah. A backhanded way of saying, "She couldn't be pretty and look like Mr. Toad here, now could she?" I *really* wanted to change the subject.

"W-What about your wife?" I asked quickly.

"Yes," sighed Phil, his face darkening as a forlorn smile spread across his lips. "My wife . . . she passed away several years ago."

My attempt at changing the subject had backfired badly.

"Uh," I fumbled, "my apologies."

"Tut-tut," said Phil with a wave of his hand. "Think nothing of it."

A long, awkward silence followed. I fidgeted nervously and dared not say another word. The conversation had hit the skids pretty fast thanks to me.

"I realize it's just speculation," Gourry piped in, "but I gotta ask. Who do you think is pulling the strings?"

In a cautious voice, Phil answered, "Christopher Ul Brozz Saillune, the Second Successor to the Royal Throne." He shook his head and covered his face with his hairy hands. "He is my younger brother."

Which brings us back to Gourry and me trying to sneak into the palace. I did feel a little sketchy, lurking around in the dark like an overambitious thief, but I still preferred it to the oppressive gloom of Mr. Gray's place. Talk about a downer—it's one thing to be the target of assassination, but it's way worse when your own brother's trying to do the assassinating.

We made sure no one was on the road before darting across like a couple of rabbits. Crouched behind the turrets of the gate, we watched the bobbing heads of the patrolling guards pass back and forth. When they reached the far sides of the gate, we rose above the wall with the help of my levitation spell.

Nice. I made sure Gourry was lying as flat as he could atop the gate before turning my head ever so slightly to check for guards.

Even nicer.

Not a single guard stood at the sentry. I made a mental note to write the palace guards a thank-you letter for their carelessness.

From where we lay, Gourry and I had a totally unobstructed and admittedly awesome view of the Royal Palace. Phil had spelled out how everything in the complex was laid out, but he couldn't help us with the positioning of the guards. I scanned the grounds to get a sense of who was on patrol and how menacing each was.

As I took in the view, I was distracted by the most ginormous temple that I'd ever laid eyes on. On either side of the temple, like minor deities attending this huge god, stood two smaller dormitories. The one on the right housed the priests, the one on the left the priestesses. Phil's daughter, Amelia, lived in the priestess' dormitory. She was supposed to be some big-time high priestess.

Behind the temple stood the equally ginormous central palace. That was where Phil used to hang his hat, er, crown, and where Clawfell and the string-puller Christopher both had their digs now.

The whole complex was so big it started to mess with my mind. One thing was for sure: you could cast a gazillion lighting spells at a gazillion different lanterns all around the courtyard and you still wouldn't be able to light more than pitiful little patches of the whole place.

Since so few guards patrolled the complex, I headed for Clawfell first. I figured Phil would sooner try to contact his own daughter before anyone else, and his enemies would, I was sure, suspect the same, landing the heavy patrols by the priestess' dormitory. Using that tack, Clawfell felt like the safer bet. And sneaking into the central palace seemed like more fun.

Am I making sense? Stop me if I'm going too fast for ya.

I turned back to Gourry, who was still face down on top of the gate. "Gourry," I whispered. "There's probably something I should tell you."

He groaned and lay his head dejectedly into his arms. "Why do I have a bad feeling about this?"

"Quit your whining. All I'm saying is if we run into trouble, don't rely on my offensive magic; my attack spells are only at about half-power in here."

He looked up at me to stare stupidly. "You mean it's *that time of the month* again?"

Men! Is that their explanation for everything? "No, dumbass!" I hissed as I tried to jab at his forehead with my boot. "My offensive magic's at half-power because of this city's layout."

"You never brought that up before," Gourry whispered back. "Why suddenly *this* city?"

Gourry's such a dunderhead most of the time, I was shocked at his sudden insistence for information.

"Uh . . . well, lots of reasons," I explained quietly. "First of all, the city's laid out like a giant six-sided ward. You know what a hexagram is, don't you?"

"It's two triangles put together," Gourry scoffed. "How dumb do you thing I am?"

It was a preschool way of describing it, but it worked.

I pointed in the direction of the palace. "The Royal Palace happens to be in the center of that giant hexagram. Still with me?"

"Yeah . . ." I noticed his mouth slowly droop open as he prepared to attempt following.

"In sorcery, a hexagram symbolizes the stable flow of power or balance. A pentagram, on the other hand, destabilizes or unbalances the natural flow of power. A pentagram represents the power of negation. You get me?"

Gourry's mouth was open so wide that I could've shoved my whole boot down his throat.

"On a small scale, without any magical amplification, a pentagram is no more powerful than a basic amulet or a ward—but if you make it massive enough, it has the same power as a humongous magical ward."

Mouth open. Eyes crossed. *Uh, Gourry?*

Whatever—I still relished blowing his mind. "Saillune City is laid out like a giant hexagram, and we're looking at the center of it. Because of the interference of the ward's field, any spell that draws on balance for power, aka White Magic spells, are amplified. On the other hand, any spell drawing its power on imbalance, like any of my attack spells, have their powers weakened. It sounds pretty bad, but lemme tell you, it could be worse. We *could* be in the middle of a banishment pentagram. That would be a major bummer."

At that point I stopped blabbering, since I could Gourry had completely checked out.

"Anyway," I said, "that's the gist of it. Got it now?"

After blinking a few times, his eyes uncrossed and his mouth closed again. "Nope," he said absently. "My bad."

At least the lunk admits he's a bit dim upstairs.

Another bit of trivia, in case you were interested, is that a White Sorcerer—a trusted adviser to the king who founded Saillune City ages ago—designed the city's layout.

Enough trivia, you say? Then back to our story.

"Well," I said, bracing myself, "let's be off."

With that, I chanted another levitation spell, and the two of us glided off the gate's ledge and onto the royal courtyard.

The scent of jasmine and lilacs filled the air, and a fresh night breeze nipped at us as we made our way into the complex. Gourry and I took note of where the guards were stationed and avoided the patches of light sent by the courtyard's lanterns.

Getting through the courtyard was the easy part—the real challenge was entering the Royal Palace. Gourry and I inspected the perimeter of the building, and every entrance was as guarded as as we'd suspected. In fact, the whole place was *crawling* with guards; whole thickets of sentries blanketed every inch of that building.

Not good. Though, I'll admit, I'm something of a thrill-seeker. Danger gets my blood pumping and the rush can get addictive after a while. Alas.

From what Phil had told us, Clawfell's room was on the third story. In any other circumstance I could've used Levitation to get us up there, but I figured floating in midair makes a fun and easy target for the guards with arrows. Quite frankly, I've never fancied the idea of becoming a pincushion.

Gourry and I crouched down behind a small hedge and tried to think.

"Hey, Lina," Gourry whispered. "Why don't you distract the guards with a magical bird call or something?"

"Can't do that," I answered. "If I summon any spells right now, it'll blow our cover in a heartbeat."

"Oh." Gourry frowned. "But what about those levitation spells you've been using? Why hasn't anyone picked up on those?"

"Levitation is a weak spell—as weak or weaker than a lighting spell," I explained. "With all these lighting spells at work around us, a levitation spell is easily camouflaged. But a summoning or attack spell? Those require a lot more power. They're detectable." I paused for a second.

"Besides," I added, "I *hate* summoning spells. I've only used 'em once."

"How come?"

"Please." I smirked. "They're not flashy enough. They undermine my style."

In the end, we took the simplest approach: Levitation, but in a roundabout way. We flew to the roof of the palace, and from there, we figured, it would be easier to avoid guards and get to Clawfell on the third story. To give you an idea: the central palace was five stories high, so the roof was high enough to be out of the guard's sight. Getting from the roof and down to the third story was going to require some delicate footwork, but Gourry and I agreed there simply wasn't another option.

Skylights lined the roof and allowed us to peer into all the rooms below. Every room seemed occupied, and we were fast getting discouraged about finding easy access into the palace . . . until we spotted one room that was completely vacant.

That's convenient, I thought. *But it feels a little too easy.*

I decided against entering through that room and instead picked a room where a plump old woman lay snoring in her cot. She looked like one of the maids, so I figured the room was a safe enough bet.

From my tunic pocket, I fished out a needle and thin steel plate and went to work on the lock that held the skylight fast.

"You haven't been holding out on me, have you?" Gourry asked with a chuckle. "You're not some ace safecracker on top of being a sorceress?" I was a little flattered by the admiring tone in his voice—a girl likes to hear a compliment every now and again, y'know.

"What are you talking about?" I answered. "I'm just your average everyday gal who knows a thing or two about picking locks."

Gourry smiled. "Liar."

Just then, I heard a click in the lock and, with a slight jerk, the skylight popped open. I took a deep breath and lowered myself into the room. Thankfully, there was a rug just below us that effectively padded the sound of our feet as we landed on the floor.

The woman didn't even stir. She kept snoring as peacefully as ever.

I tiptoed to the door and pressed my ear against the oak, careful to listen for any noises from the corridor. After hearing nothing, I slowly turned the handle and pulled the door open.

The corridor was quiet and ran straight on either side. Dimly lit torches placed in brackets dotted the stone walls, and a lone guard sat slumped nearby. In fact, he was stationed by the door of the empty room that we'd spotted from the roof. It *was* a trap as I'd suspected, although it wasn't a very good one as proven by the snoozing soldier.

Sleeping on duty. Thanks for the help, soldier!

Fortunately for us, there weren't many other guards

around. We didn't spot a single one as we made our way to the stairway at the end of the corridor and down a flight of stairs. But as we peered around the bend that led to another flight, we saw the shadows of guards against the walls and heard a low murmur coming from the corridor.

Drat.

I cursed more colorfully in my head, but I'd already known we'd have to deal with soldiers sooner or later. Besides, we were on the floor where that string-puller Christopher slept—more guards was no surprise.

With a wave of my hand, I cast a sleeping spell on the sentries. We watched as the guards' shadows dropped one by one.

A minute or two of super-sneaking later, we found ourselves on Clawfell's floor. We'd barely encountered any resistance. I know, I know—sounds fantastic, right? But it didn't feel that way; the ease of our entry stuck to the roof of my mouth like a gob of yak paste. It felt wrong.

The corridor was strangely quiet. We grabbed the hilts of our swords, ready for anything that might pounce from the shadows, and began gingerly making our way down the corridor.

"What do you think?" I asked Gourry hesitantly.

He shook his head. "I don't like it," he whispered back. "It feels like a trap."

"We've come too far to turn back now." I grabbed him by the arm and said quietly, "Listen, when we find Clawfell's room, let's not rush into anything. Stay quiet and let me figure out if it's really him first."

"Gotcha," Gourry answered. "I'll leave the gabbing to you."

I figured that if Christopher was cunning enough, he might've moved Clawfell to another room and replaced the aide with an impostor. Gourry and I might've played right into Christopher's greedy little hands. After finding the door that supposedly led to Clawfell's room, I began picking the lock as carefully as I could. It snapped open with barely a hitch; we slid into the room and shut the door behind us.

Half the bedroom was cloaked in darkness. The other half, bathed in soft moonlight that filtered through the window, held an ornate wooden bed on which we spied a sleeping old man. He certainly fit the description Phil gave us, but we needed a closer look. Besides, looking like Clawfell didn't mean he really *was* Clawfell.

I quietly drew my sword. Clutching it in one hand, I tiptoed up to him and firmly clamped my other hand over the man's mouth.

The geezer's eyes snapped open. Panic-stricken, he muffled a cry and tried to wriggle free from under my arm. He didn't have much luck.

That's my sword-fightin' arm, kids, and it's awfully strong.

I tipped the blade of my sword toward his chin. Then, in the most intimidating voice I could muster, I hissed, "Don't raise your voice." Once he finally gave up trying to break free, I eased up on him and withdrew my hand from his mouth.

"Clawfell?" I asked him brusquely. He tried to gulp down a lump of terror wedged in his throat and kept his wide eyes fixed on mine.

"Are you assassins . . . sent from Christopher?!" he asked feebly.

That was a good sign. If the guy had been a fake, he would've more likely said, "This is all a misunderstanding!" or something lame like that.

I gave Gourry an approving nod and straightened up, sheathing my sword.

Clawfell propped himself up on an elbow and wiped his sore mouth with one hand. He eyed us suspiciously.

"Didn't mean to hurt or startle you," I said. "We just had to make sure you're the real deal."

He cocked his head and asked warily, "Who are you people?"

Gourry stepped forward. "We come with a message from Philionel," he said as self-importantly as he could probably manage.

Clawfell sat up in amazement. "His Excellency?!" he cried.

"Shh!" I hissed. "Quiet!"

Clawfell halted and bit his lip contritely.

I sighed.

Please tell me nobody heard that squeal.

"He just wanted to let you and Amelia know that he was safe and sound."

"I see," he responded, his voice quavering with joy as he clasped his hands. "Thank the gods His Excellency is safe."

He sounded like he was about to break down and cry. I felt sorry for the codger—he looked pretty lonely.

Clawfell gazed up at us with eager eyes. "And where is His Excel—? No, wait. It's best if I do not know where he is."

"Yeah," I agreed. "We'd like you to pass the message along to Amelia. We thought about sneaking into her dormitory quarters, but it's way too risky."

"I certainly shall," he said. He gripped my arm urgently. "As for you, you must return immediately. There's no reason to stay any longer. And tell his Excellency to be careful and to not worry about us."

"Gotcha," I whispered. "We'll be on our way."

We backed out of the room, leaving him sitting up in bed, his mouth agape and the hem of his nightgown flapping in the breeze. Gourry and I made sure the coast was clear and slid out into the corridor.

Our escape route was easy enough: just backtrack the way we came. We made it to the stairway and began climbing.

At least, it *was* easy enough. Until we heard the—

KA-BOOM!

The floor and walls shook violently; Gourry and I grabbed hold of each other to keep from falling backward down the stairs.

"What happened?!" one guard shouted.

"What the hell was that noise?!"

"Gary, what'd you do *this* time?!"

"Don't panic!" That sounded like a guard leader. "Return to your posts! Stand your ground 'til we receive word from the officers outside!"

Alarmed screams and commotion totally took over the corridors above and below us. We didn't want to stick around for a guard to show up in the stairway, so we lurched ahead toward the upper stories. Moments later we managed to scramble onto the topmost floor.

For all the pell-mell going on around her, the old woman kept snoring like a hibernating grizzly.

While I have to admit my curiosity was piqued by the sudden rush of activity in the palace, my first priority was getting us out of there. I chanted Levitation and grabbed Gourry's hand before ascending through the skylight. Once on the roof, I replaced the skylight in its frame. I wasn't able to lock it up again, but under the circumstances, who the hell was gonna care?

We'll levitate out of here, I thought, *and we'll be out of this mess in no time.* No sooner had I thought that than Gourry nudged me from behind.

"Don't look now, Lina." Gourry made a sound in the back of his throat like a tiger's growl and drew his sword.

Above us, just hanging in midair, was a lone man in flowing robes. I should've known my luck couldn't last.

"Is there something I can do for you?" the floating man said calmly.

With that great big canopy of stars behind his long, flapping mantle, I must say he cut quite a dashing figure. If it weren't for a nasty scar that ran down his right cheek and the icy expression in his eyes, I might've found him pretty hot. There was a sinister glittering in his pupils, and a curl in his thin lips that said, "I've been a bad, bad boy."

The guy knew we were sneaking around inside and had been waiting for us to show up; he set off pandemonium among the guards so he could distract them and corner us alone up on the roof.

Whatever his reasons, something told me that flight— not fight—was the better option this time.

"Ray Wing!" I grabbed onto Gourry as my high-speed flight spell kicked into full gear. I'd have that evil sorcerer with his levitation spell eating my dust in mere seconds. Ray Wing's wind barrier surrounded us like a force field against Flare Arrows and other nasty bits of offensive magic.

But I was foiled again! Just after we began to speed away, I ran into a shockwave.

WHACK!

It rammed straight into my Wind Barrier with such a jolt that it knocked my brains loose for a second. I managed to snap out of it and regain my midair balance. The force of the impact had sent us hurling down toward the courtyard, and I barely kept us from plowing right into a rush of startled and scurrying guards.

Fortunately for me and Gourry, the Wind Barrier held fast. If it had shattered from the collision with the shockwave, both of us would've been pulverized instantly.

A shockwave plus a levitation spell equals a sorcerer who is by no means an amateur.

Meanwhile, the guards running amok in the courtyard had caught on to what was happening far above them. They screamed in terror as we screeched through the pitch black of night like a couple of human meteors. Wide-eyed and dumbfounded, they pointed and gawked as I tried to keep control of our descent.

"What the . . . what *is* that?!" cried one of 'em.

"Intruders!" another yelled.

Intruders?! Well, duh!

I tried to slow down so our impact with the ground wouldn't be too traumatic. I didn't have much luck.

"Ow-ow-ow!" yelled Gourry as he bounced and tumbled across the lawn.

"Dammit!" I hissed as I skidded to a stop palms-first. My side was bruised, my ankle hurt, and I had the wind knocked out of me. *You* try getting hit with a shockwave and see how well you do.

We groaned in pain and somehow managed to scramble back to our feet.

"Identify yourselves!" yelled the captain of the guards. I could tell by his shaking knees that we'd scared him silly, but he tried to sound all strong and authoritative.

Gourry, who was doubled over and trying to catch his breath, waved to the enclosing guards to sheath their swords.

"Don't worry," he insisted between pants. "We're not suspicious at all."

By habit, he'd unsheathed his own sword and was holding it semi-aloft in his right hand. So his pleas to the others to put away their weapons weren't exactly convincing.

"I entreat you, Captain Razes."

It was the sorcerer's voice. He hung in the air not far above the courtyard, lowering himself with slow, deliberate grace to show how in control of the elements he was. His feet touched the ground noiselessly, and, with that icy smile, he stalked toward us and cooed, "Leave their fate to me."

Razes sneered at him incredulously. "Is that you, Kanzeil?" Displeasure twisted the captain's face, like he'd just sat on a banana cream cake. "This is a matter for the Royal Guards," he growled.

Just then, an approaching voice interrupted with, "Let him do as he likes, Razes."

I looked in the direction of the Royal Palace and saw two figures, half-hidden in the shadows, striding our way.

I didn't know who they were, but one thing was for sure: the guy leading the way was really good-looking and impeccably groomed. Okay, he might've been a tad old for me; I put him at around forty, but he had a tight, slender build. He also had soft dark eyes, unlike the sorcerer's evil-looking peepers. Someone younger followed just behind him—his son, maybe, and from where I was standing, he looked just as tight as daddy.

My, it's turning out to be a stellar night for man watching.

"But sir!" Razes implored of the older, distinguished-looking gentleman. "These two are our prisoners!"

"Razes, you're the captain of the Royal Guards, are you not?" The handsome man arched an eyebrow. "And, being as such, are you not subordinate to me?"

The captain looked dumbfounded for a moment. He finally lowered his head with an air of resignation.

In the few seconds I'd been standing there, I'd picked up a couple of hunches in regards to the handsome forty-year-old:

#1: He could be a little foul tempered.

#2: He could be Christopher.

"Very good," Kanzeil said silkily. He extended his right hand toward us. "It would be my high honor to kill them both."

And, just like that, he began chanting a spell.

Slow down! His honor would do what now?

I thought the conversation would go on for a while, like maybe he'd start babbling filler garbage like: "I shall capture these two and learn where Philionel is hiding at last!" and cackle maniacally while I whipped up an escape plan. But the evil-looking sorcerer skipped all the courtesies and went right into killing mode. It's safe to say Gourry and I were a bit stunned, and the impeccably groomed gentleman looked every bit as shocked as we.

"W-wait, Kanzeil!" Christopher shouted as he reached out. "What are you—?!"

A light emerged from Kanzeil's right hand and began gathering power rapidly. He'd rattled off his chant awfully fast. "Perish!" he boomed, extending his trembling hand toward us. A flare leaped from his palm, but Kanzeil was too late. In the split second the middle-aged guy had yapped at him, I had released a levitation spell, trying to time it with Kanzeil's chanting. My plan worked out brilliantly if I do say so myself.

I grabbed hold of Gourry and took off just as Kanzeil's flare flew through where we'd been. Arcing through the air, I guided us straight for the south gate before Kanzeil had a chance to regroup and unleash another shot.

Unfortunately, it didn't quite go as smoothly as I'd have liked.

VUUN!

With a howling echo, a red beam slammed into my Wind Barrier, sending us somersaulting through the air. I managed to regain control of my course and keep a hold on Gourry.

"Ow!" Gourry suddenly cried.

I glanced over at him. "What happened?" I shouted.

"My leg." He grunted and winced. "B-but it's just a graze. Don't worry, just go!"

I was worried. He might've claimed it was a graze, but I knew he was probably downplaying the wound; the wince on his face gave him away. I ground my teeth together and tried to think.

That magic beam couldn't have come from Kanzeil. So who else fired that second shot?

The beam had been powerful enough to punch through the Wind Barrier, so whoever had cast it was no lightweight.

"Just hang on," I consoled Gourry. "We'll be back in no time."

With that, I soared across the palace grounds as fast as I could toward Mr. Gray's house.

***

"And that brings us to now," I concluded. I sighed and relaxed back in my chair. In the parlor back at Mr. Gray's, I took another sip from my cup of black tea and let Mr. Gray and Phil digest all that I'd divulged.

I glanced uncomfortably at Gourry's half-bandaged foot. Some of his flesh had been seared by the blast, and Mr. Gray was still tending to it as the sun began to rise over the city.

Phil shook head as he paced. "I'm sorry for putting you through such trouble," he murmured. "And now, on top of that," he paused and gestured toward Gourry's foot, "suffering injury."

"It was nothin'," Gourry strained to say lightheartedly from his lying position on a divan. We all knew it was more serious than Gourry led on; he wasn't fooling anybody. Fortunately, the magic beam had only grazed Gourry's foot and missed all the bones, *and* Mr. Gray was a magic powder-and-potion healer of considerable skill, so Gourry wasn't going to sustain any long-term damage. That still didn't make me feel much better.

"So that decently attractive older guy . . ." I cleared my throat and looked away from Gourry. "He really was Christopher, huh?" Phil nodded heavily. "Yes," he said. "He resembles me greatly, don't you think."

Uh . . . whatever you say, pops.

"And the younger guy with him . . . that was his son?"

"Indeed," Phil replied, pouring tea into an empty cup. "The boy you saw was Chris's son, Alfred." Phil stirred sugar into his tea and began to sip. "But he's not the problem. Kanzeil is the problem."

Kanzeil certainly *was* the problem. That maniac had nearly burnt us to a crisp.

"Christopher claims that Kanzeil is an old friend. But, of course, that cannot be so; all this trouble began after Chris invited Kanzeil to the Royal Palace."

Gourry sat up, propped on his elbows. "So you think the assassins are taking their orders straight from Christopher?"

Phil gazed into the gray morning light. "As awful as it sounds, yes. First, he brings a snake into the Royal Palace in the form of Kanzeil—someone who only encourages his own evil ambitions. Then, he dispatches assassins not only at me but at my most trusted allies." It was clear Phil's heart was breaking even as he spoke. "How can I forgive him? My own brother!"

A long silence hung over us before I finally asked Phil, "What will you do now?"

My question snapped Phil out of his grim thoughts.

"Well," he pondered, "as I said before, I need to obtain definitive proof from of Christopher's hand in all this. But sneaking back in so soon after your escape is perhaps not the wisest idea."

"Definitely not," I seconded.

Phil gulped the rest of his tea, set his cup down, and began pacing the parlor again with his tubby arms folded.

I'd never seen anyone pace around so much. He was one jittery guy, and watching him was making my head spin.

Phil finally slumped into a chair, clutching his forehead with his hand. "The question is, *when* to breech the palace."

THUD!

The door in the hallway had been slammed shut by panicky hands.

"Something terrible has happened!" Maria cried as she staggered into the parlor. She tottered to a chair near the doorway, her face blanched.

"Maria?" Mr. Gray asked, alarmed.

"I just heard . . . a pronouncement from . . . the Royal Palace," she wheezed between pants. "Last night, Lord Clawfell was arrested for conspiracy to assassinate the king."

"What?!" we all cried at once.

"Lord Clawfell is the prime instigator in the current string of assassinations. Prince Christopher has vowed to punish Clawfell to the fullest extent!" Maria covered her face with her hands and broke into panicked sobs.

"Damn him!" Phil roared. "He's trying to bait me by threatening to harm my friends!"

"I'm sorry," Gourry uttered. "This is all 'cause we were spotted last night."

"It's not your fault at all." Phil walked to the window again, and, slowly, I saw his eyebrows furrow grimly.

"The time has come to act," he declared.

"Okay," Gourry said, rising to his feet, "But let us come with you. After all, the enemy arrested Clawfell right after we broke in; we can't just march out of here with a 'Good luck with the mess we helped put you in, bye-bye!' "

He was right. For a doofus, Gourry could make a pretty good diplomatic point.

Phil nodded graciously. "I thank you," he said.

I took a breath and stood from my chair. *Okay,* I thought, cracking my knuckles. *Here we go again.*

"Open the gates!" Phil bellowed at the top of his lungs. "It is I, Philionel Di Saillune!!"

For a geezer, he sure had a set of pipes.

A soldier on the lookout saw us and bolted. Not long after, the heavy front gates of the Royal Palace creaked open before us.

Without hesitation, Phil marched in. Gourry and I kept in step behind him.

Phil wore his silken regal robe that day. It didn't have much gold embroidery on it, but it did have the insignia of the royal crest. Still, a girl's gotta be honest: the fancy attire didn't suit Phil *at all*. It was like putting a dress on a bulldog. You catch get my drift?

Gourry had this flax jerkin on that Mr. Gray had picked out for him. It was lovely . . . as far as jerkins go. Over that, he wore his breastplate with the sign of the iron serpent on it, and his long sword hung at his hip.

As for me, I wore black trousers and a new robe I'd picked up in one of Saillune's markets. A black mantle, woven from mythril fibers, clung to my shoulders, flanked by heavily reinforced gold-plated shoulder guards made of ground dragonbone. To top off my look, I wore my black bandanna, short sword, and my holiest of possessions—my jewel-encrusted amulet.

Okay, so maybe I went a bit overboard, but it isn't every day that you get to escort a prince to his palatial digs.

"And who are these two, sire?" asked the soldier who greeted us.

"Allies," Phil answered tersely. His sole intention was to confront Christopher, and he was determined to proceed.

"His Excellency!" one soldier yelled.

"His Excellency has returned!" announced another.

Phil halted mid-stride, recognizing someone standing at the foot of the temple steps. From our distance, it looked like one of the priestesses. She suddenly let loose with a long, exulted cry.

"Daaaddyyy! You're home!"

The priestess lifted the hem of her robe and ran daintily toward Phil's outstretched arms. Halfway there, she less-daintily tripped.

Okay, I'll tell you straight: she was cute. She wasn't much older than me and had raven shoulder-length hair. She had big, beautiful eyes and a fair complexion. The only flaw I could make out (at least, on first impression—but give me time) was that her priestess' robe was a couple of sizes too big for her. Oddly enough, the way it draped and flowed all over made her look that much cuter.

To her benefit, she didn't look a mite like her father.

"Amelia!" Phil cried, his face beaming. "How've you been?"

"Sheesh! I'm fine, Father," Amelia gushed. "And I knew you were too!"

Phil hugged her. "Now," he asked dotingly, "are you telling me you knew all along I was safe?"

"I sure am," she answered. "Know why? 'Cause justice always wins in the end."

Uh, girl, we gotta talk. I got news for ya.

She turned her gaze to Gourry and me.

"And who're these two?" she asked.

"Ah!" Phil spun around to face us. "This is Miss Lina and Mr. Gourry, my allies."

Phil kept an arm gently around Amelia's shoulders. "Here she is," he declared with pride. "My second daughter."

"Second?" I blurted without thinking.

"Yes, my elder daughter is Gracia. She's off right now on one of her training journeys. She hasn't returned yet."

"Big Sis is probably just lost like usual," Amelia said with a big smile.

Bingo.

Phil tucked a strand of hair behind Amelia's ear and stroked her face. "If I do say so myself," he remarked, "she's quite a beauty. Just like her father."

Gourry and I couldn't help but exchange a pained glance.

"Nice to meet you!" Amelia said perkily. She shot a hand up in greeting and smiled so widely it made the muscles around *my* mouth sore. I wondered if that sort of chipperness was the result of medication.

"Y-Yeah," said Gourry. "You too."

Amelia shuffled in her robes; her smile still beaming from her face. Something suddenly caught her eye.

"Oh!" she exclaimed. "Looks like Uncle's here to welcome you too." Three figures, still shadowy, emerged from the entrance to the temple. They descended the wide steps and approached us.

True to cryptic form, it was the trio who'd greeted us so memorably the night before: the middle-aged feller we now knew to be Christopher, his son Alfred, and Kanzeil the Sorcerer.

"Brother," Christopher oozed, his arms outstretched. "You're safe?"

A bitter look hardened over Phil's face. "Of course I am."

An awkward moment passed, in which Christopher, realizing that Phil didn't want a hug from him, grudgingly lowered his arms. "Where of all places have you been?" Christopher eventually asked. "I was worried sick about you." Christopher's tone was suspicious to say the least. He surely sensed that Phil was on to him, but he still kept right on, probably to see how far he could go before Phil told him to drop the act.

Of course, Christopher spotted us, and asked with the same mock-ignorance, "And the two you've brought with you?"

No matter how long we kept up these niceties, there was no getting around it: here we were, the two infiltrators from last night, now reentering the palace in the company of the rightful heir. Put the pieces together, and you can see what a dicey situation Gourry and I had gotten ourselves into.

"Oh, you mean these guys?" Amelia jumped in. She didn't smile this time. "They're *old friends* of Father's."

Old friends? Oh, right—the same excuse Christopher had made with Kanzeil. The battle lines were getting drawn, all right.

A flat, stammered, "I see . . ." was all Christopher could come up with as a response.

"This is Miss Lina Inverse," Phil explained calmly, "and that is Mr. Gourry Gabriev."

Kanzeil furrowed his brows intently. *"You* are Lina Inverse?"

My reputation precedes me, I guess. By the stunned look on his face, I assumed Kanzeil had only heard the notorious stuff.

That's right. I'm dangerous, so step off!

"Silence, Kanzeil," Chrisopher snapped.

"Forgive me." Kanzeil slinked back a few steps, his head lowered.

It was some act those guys were putting on. If Kanzeil had been in the mood, he could've vaporized Christopher with a snap of his fingers. And, for his part, Christopher only wanted the facial-scarred Kanzeil around to accommodate his power bid. Not the cuddliest of friendships, I gathered.

"Let me, Father," Amelia suddenly said. She turned toward us, made a grand sweep of an arm, and declared, "This is Christopher, my *beloved* uncle!"

Christopher looked pained. If I didn't know any better, I'd have said he was in dire need of a laxative.

"And this is Alfred," Amelia continued cheerfully. "And that's my uncle's old friend, Kanzeil. Things in the Royal Palace started getting messy *right after* he was invited in, but I'm sure that was just an unfortunate coincidence!"

I sincerely doubted Amelia was trying to be sarcastic, but she made her remarks loud enough for the gathered soldiers to get an earful. I sensed they were already suspicious about Christopher, since they pointedly sneered at him once Amelia was done.

"It's nice to see you again," I said confidently. "Oh, did I say *again?* Because I met for the first time *ever,* sorry."

I heard Gourry choke back a giggle. I could see Christopher's agitation grow, but he still kept up his tack of appearing gracious and relieved to see his brother again.

"Well, I'm just glad you're safe," he murmured to Phil. "If you'll excuse us, we'll take our leave."

He spun around on his heels and began to skulk away. Phil's cry stopped him.

"Wait, Chris!"

Christopher cringed and slowly turned around with the most uptight expression on his face.

Someone, please, get this man some bran!

"Yes, my dear Brother?" he hissed.

"Release Clawfell," Phil demanded. "Now!"

Christopher shook his head sternly. "I can't do that," he said, a cruel smile spreading over his lips. "We have information that Clawfell convened secretly with intruders last night. You'll thank me for arresting him, Brother, for I believe he's centrally involved in the conspiracy to assassinate you."

"Stop your blathering," Phil snarled as he pointed at Gourry and me. "These were the messengers who met him, and they are my friends!"

"Th—!" The words caught in Christopher's throat, and the scowl on his face stiffened. Christopher, I'm sure, thought he could dance around the issues and be gone, but Phil was really holding his feet in the fire. It surprised me as much as it did Christopher.

"Messengers?" Christopher asked. "For what purpose?"

"My messengers contacted Clawfell in secret last night." Phil put his hands on his hips. "They informed me that, on their way back, they were intercepted by a sorcerer and barely escaped a fireball. Now I ask you this: Don't you think the sorcerer and those he is in league with are more likely to be the conspirators against me?"

Christopher's mouth fell open.

"Clawfell is not to blame." Phil, his hands balled into fists, approached Christopher until he was inches away from his nose. "Release him . . . now!"

"B-But . . ." Christopher blubbered.

"But *what?!*"

"Is it true . . . what you say?"

A sly smile spread across Phil's squat face. "Surely you're not implying that I'm covering for Clawfell? Why would I do that? Unless you think that I might be the one the pulling the strings, orchestrating a series of plots to assassinate *myself*?" Phil threw Christopher's warped logic right back at him. "Is that what you really think, Brother?"

Christopher was left speechless. He blinked a couple of times and finally blurted, "Of course not!" He was red-faced and shaken, and Gourry and I were loving it.

"Good. Then we agree—release Clawfell," Phil ordered. "I must be off."

"Let me help, Father," Amelia chirped giddily. "Let me help!"

Phil turned to Gourry and me.

"I must attend to some business here at the palace," he said. "It's unavoidable, I'm afraid. Would someone here be good enough to show my friends around the premises while I'm engaged?"

That got me a little worried. Was it a good idea for Phil to go off alone somewhere, without the only two people he could trust? But then I figured it was broad daylight: who in their right mind would attack Phil at that hour, especially with his guards and courtiers everywhere? Besides, from what I'd just seen, Christopher was a wuss—all bark and no bite.

While I was mulling that over, Kanzeil stepped forward. "If it please thee, sire," he said smoothly, "I would be happy to show our guests around."

After trying to barbeque us the night before?! I don't think so.

But, like Amelia and Phil, I stuck with our game plan.

"Thanks ever so much," I said, smiling as sweetly as I could. "So pleased to make your acquaintance."

We climbed an ornate staircase made of polished white augite and passed through a massive archway. Magnificent stained glass mosaics lined the walls, depicting the various monarchs who had ruled Saillune City through the centuries.

Not to sound artsy-fartsy here, but it was some of the most amazing artwork I'd ever seen. It wasn't gaudy, but it wasn't plain; the pictures were a perfect balance of majesty and modesty. A rich crimson carpet stretched toward the grand altar.

But I'm gonna stop now, because I sound like a fop.

"This is the temple dedicated to Sylpheed, the Red Dragon," Kanzeil explained, his voice echoing through the room. "Here is where all the coronations and royal weddings are held." His tone seemed oddly disinterested. "The structures to the left and right of us are the dormitories. Priestesses reside in the left, and priests in the right . . . and I think that's all that needs to be said about that.

"Guests are not allowed to enter the dormitories," he explained in a hushed tone, "so we shall cross to the other side of the temple through here and on to the central palace."

Kanzeil strode quickly through the temple, barely bothering to point out anything. I tried to take in the fabulous sculptures and tapestries that hung high above the arched windows, while Gourry just rushed through with his mouth open, looking upward.

Kanzeil, more than anything, just seemed bored and distracted. I already expected him to be rubbing in remarks about how powerful he was and how he could destroy both of us in a heartbeat if he wanted to. You know, the standard threats you expect to hear from an evil jerk.

I was willing to bide our time and see what he had up those ultra-wide sleeves of his. We walked through a glass-roofed passageway that led into the palace, and looking up through transparent panels, I caught a glimpse of the clear, blue sky.

If it hadn't been for the fairly tense (not to mention irritating) situation that I found myself in, I'd have slowed down to really enjoy the morning. Maybe I'd have taken a leisurely stroll through the palace gardens and sat by the fountains. It made me realize how much I needed a nap. After a few minutes of daydreaming, I suddenly noticed Kanzeil hotfooting through and opening some serious distance between us. Gourry and I picked up our pace to catch up . . . but just then, I felt the weirdest sensation.

No matter how fast we walked, we couldn't catch up with Kanzeil. As I wondered how he could be getting farther and farther away from us, he suddenly vanished. I froze, and whipped around to Gourry.

He had vanished with Kanzeil.

Damn it all to hell.

I'd fallen for that asshole sorcerer's spell.

2 : WHY ME?!
WHAT DID I DO?!

I jerked my head around to look behind me. The passageway seemed as if it stretched on for forever, disappearing into blackness. I gritted my teeth, unable to see neither the temple nor the palace anymore.

Warped space.

The first thing that went through my head was simple: Was a spell like that really possible? In theory, I supposed it was. Summoning spells manipulate space by folding it to accommodate whatever's summoned, but a spell that messed up space *that* bad? Yeesh.

I had to resist the spell and test its limits somehow. The corridor didn't have any banisters, but it was laid out with stout pillars that supported the roof. On either side were green lawns, made endless by the spell I was swiftly growing to hate.

Okay, I'll admit—I was getting a little freaked. I took a deep breath and tried to stay calm. "All right," I said to myself. "Just think, Lina. *Think.*"

The lawns were only slightly less menacing than the neverending path, but I didn't know where else to start. I took a careful step on the grass.

I suddenly found myself standing in the middle of the corridor again. Apparently the wielder of the spell had physical control of my movements as well.

"Damn," I snarled. "No fair."

I scrambled for a solution: a mode of action, a strategy, anything. While I stood there, trying desperately to come up with something plausible, I heard footsteps.

So that was it. This was the space for our showdown. The footsteps echoed through the passageway—loud, like the beating of giant drums, and more intimidating than a cavalry charge. Whoever was heading my way was no pipsqueak.

I wasn't all that excited about the imminent confrontation, but I figured I didn't have much of a choice. So, I fell to doing the only thing I *could* do: I began chanting a spell.

It was originally meant, in the strictest sense, to summon a gargoyle—you know, a winged creature hewn out of magic rock. But I was varying the chant a bit in hopes of summoning something a little different. You see, once you know your way around your spells, you can start improvising and modulating them according to your needs.

I continued reciting the chants, trying not to pay attention to the footsteps that steadily drew nearer. My eyes snapped open as I completed my incantation.

There!

A dainty, white bird appeared from my hands. It poked its beak at the air for a couple of seconds, then flapped its wings and fluttered away into the brilliant morning sunshine.

"A dove," Gourry muttered as he watched it fly. "How cute." The space I stood in had abruptly returned to normal.

Ladies and gentlemen, Lina Inverse kicks ass.

I hurried up to Gourry, my feet pattering along the marble floor. "Looks like it worked," I muttered.

"What worked?" Gourry asked once I'd caught up.

"Nothing." I figured I'd better keep what had just happened to myself, lest Gourry think I was pulling his leg or, even worse, going bonkers.

I didn't want to get into a conversation about space manipulation with Gourry—not now, not ever.

What I'd summoned through my chant was indeed a regular white dove. The instant that normal space came in contact with the warped space of the corridor, the warping spell broke. You see, whenever real space and unreal space collide with each other, real space always wins; connecting a fake world to the real world means bye-bye to Crazy Land.

Of course, there are exceptions to everything. My intuitive slickness had been aided with a little luck. "Not bad, Kanzeil," I playfully told the creep. "Not bad at all."

"What do you mean by that?" Kanzeil's tone and expression were totally deadpan.

You ain't foolin' anybody, wizard-man, leastwise Lina.

It was a rocky but adventurous start to our stay at the Royal Palace.

***

It was peaceful that night, with crickets chirping in the courtyard and the moon casting gentle light into my room. I lay in bed, relaxing for the first time that day and enjoying the night breeze that drifted in from the windows. My body ached, my nerves were shot, and I was ready for a long snooze.

Gourry and I had separate adjoining guest rooms, both just down the hall from Phil. It was nice to have a room all to myself; often, I ended up sharing cramped and stinky quarters with Gourry at rundown inns while journeying here or there. Still, I couldn't get carried away with the room's tempting comforts—Gourry and I were on a mission, so I had to be alert should anything go awry with Phil during the night.

Sure, Phil had guards and soldiers posted all over the place, but Gourry and I were personally responsible for watching over him. The rewards in the form of grub and money promised to be excellent, so we accepted without too much arm-twisting. I was *hoping* the palace guards could handle any crises that might come up (and my job would end up cushy), but I doubted it. Weren't those the same guards Gourry and had I slid past totally undetected? We'd even found one of them dozing at his post.

I sighed and rolled over.

Chalk it up to feminine intuition, but I couldn't shake the feeling that something was about to happen. I also had the feeling it was going to happen to *me*. The crickets seemed to catch wind of it first, because all of a sudden, their chirping stopped.

I turned my eyes to the downturned slats of my window shutters. And blinked.

A person-shaped shadow stood in the rays of the moonlight. First, I thought it was just my imagination: my anxieties were getting the better of me. I rubbed my eyes a few times, but the shape was still there.

How the hell did he get up here?

My room was three floors up, and it didn't have a verandah.

In one quick movement, I rolled out of bed and grabbed the sword from my sheath. Whoever—or whatever—was out there had the same thing in mind, because a blade cut vertically through the rows of slats in one deft sweep, ripping through them like they were strips of paper. Wedges and chunks of wood went flying and clattering everywhere.

A gust of wind howled. Framed by the window, stood a humanlike figure clad completely in black and clutching a sword.

"You chose the wrong gal on the wrong night to pick a fight with, buddy!" I tried to sound as tough as I could under the circumstances.

The assassin stepped in through the window. His feet were noiseless as they touched and crossed the floor, and I could see nothing of him except the glint of his eyes through the slits in his mask. Most incredibly, I couldn't sense his presence; it was like he wasn't even there.

"Sneaking into a girl's room in the middle of a night," I snapped. "Where'd you learn your manners?" The figure didn't speak, just approached me slowly. "Least you could do is tell me your name."

Through his mask, he spoke a single word: "Zuuma."

That was easy. Usually, I gotta pull teeth to get the names of my enemies—literally.

His obliging nature caught me off guard. "I'm impressed, Zuuma. For an assassin, you're very polite."

Zuuma raised his sword. "Only two know my name," he bellowed. "My master . . . and my prey."

Great. One-liners.

The wind rose again and circled the room.

I knew, with a wall several steps behind me, and a nightstand to my left; my only escape route was to my right.

And Zuuma knew it too.

Of course, he was thinking of heading me off once I made my move, so I feinted to my right. He jumped forward and I leapt on my bed. I took that split-second to start chanting a spell. Zuuma somersaulted in midair, planted his feet on the far wall, and shot toward me. Luckily, I managed to dodge him again, but I heard him chanting a spell under his breath. All I could detect was that it didn't sound like an attack spell.

In spell-to-spell combat, you have to be able to anticipate your opponent's spell well beforehand. It's not so hard once you get used to it: you know which spells are best deployed at any given moment in combat, and you can detect, by listening closely enough, generally what kind of spell your opponent is chanting from its very rhythm. Sounds complicated, but if you're as battle-hardened as I am, it's second nature.

When you start mixing in physical combat with spell-to-spell, that's when things can get a little hairy. Zuuma seemed pretty smooth at it—he landed on the far side of the room and, with a determined grunt, tossed his sword aside and stomped toward me with clenched fists.

So he wanted to go at it hand-to-hand, eh? He probably thought that because he'd abandoned his weapon I'd do the same, and we'd move on to wrestling like a pair of uneducated grunts. The idea didn't sound too appealing, so I held fast to the sword in my hand, ready to swing if he dove at me again.

The fact that all this was happening in the dim light of the moon made things a bit more exhilarating. I figured I'd attack him with the spell I was chanting, and, if that didn't faze him; I'd blind him with a lighting spell, but that was about as far as I got in my thought process.

Just then, I heard a pounding on the door.

"Lina!" came Gourry's voice through the wood. "Is something wrong?!" He pounded again.

I fought hard not to roll my eyes.

Is something wrong? No, Gourry, it's just my buddy Zuuma and we're just messin' around. Don't mind us!

"Gourry!" I yelled. "You're gonna have to break through!"

He was fiddling with the bolt, but, like the smarty-pants I am, I'd locked the door before going to bed. Unless I fancied a close encounter with Zuuma's fists, I had no way of dashing for the door to open it.

I finished chanting my spell and threw up my arms. "Bram Blazer!" I yelled as a shockwave of light blasted from my hands. Zuuma evaded it like he was skipping around a puddle. The trail of light zoomed out the window and vanished in the night air.

Zuuma crouched down and growled, "Dark Mist!" I'd just registered Zuuma's low, gravelly voice when everything around me went black.

SHOOM.

At least before I'd had the moonlight. Now it was as if a hand had passed over the sky and darkened the whole earth.

A very *big* hand that wanted me dead.

"Wha—?!" I cried out.

The complete blackness was pretty unsettling, but I needed to strategize pretty damn fast. I chanted rapidly.

"Lighting!" I called out. I extended the palm of my hand, waving it in a circular pattern to release a swath of light in every direction. Except, there wasn't light, only an inky-looking wave. Whatever spell Zuuma had summoned, it didn't just block light—it sapped light from any and all light sources within its field. Not only that, but I couldn't sense my opponent's presence.

He's masking himself again.

I clenched the hilt of my sword tightly. Where was he lurking in the infuriating blackness? Of course, Zuuma couldn't see me either, but he could definitely sense me.

The next instant, any icy chill ran up my spine. I instinctively spun around and slashed my sword at whatever was behind me.

Something touched my neck.

Splish! I heard a wet, squelching sound just as I felt a stabbing pain in my throat.

"Lina!" came Gourry's shout. I heard the violent splintering of wood, then the loud thunk of his sword striking the floor. "Lina, are you—huh?!"

Gourry charged into the room, startled momentarily by the pitch blackness. A second later, after sensing my presence, he ran right for me and grabbed me by the shoulders. He shook me so hard my teeth rattled.

"Lina!" he cried. "Are you okay?! Who did this—is he still here?!"

I clutched his wrist to get him to stop shaking me.

I can hear just fine. You don't have to scream.

"Lina?"

Relief suddenly flooded through me. I couldn't muster the words to tell him how glad I was to see him, so I just buried my face in his chest and nodded silently.

Gourry's voice calmed. "You're okay," he said gently. "I think the guy bolted." He lifted my chin and fixed his eyes on mine. "Are you really all right?"

I managed a moan, but nothing more as pain seared my throat. Zuuma had just about crushed my windpipe. A moment later, and he would've succeeded.

"A-a-a-a-ahh . . . n-night . . . r-r-I . . . am Lina In . . . v-verse . . ." I sputtered.

Gourry looked at me like I was either insane or possessed. Or both.

I was just trying out my voice to make sure it still worked.

Zuuma was gone, and light had returned to the room. Gourry went out to explain what happened to one of the guards. Afterward he took me to the temple so that magic healers could tend to me immediately.

The healers seemed unperturbed considering they'd just been woken up in the middle of the night on a life-or-death errand. Actually, they were calm and poised as they mixed magic herbs in a broth to heal my throat.

I'd have thanked them right away if only I could've talked.

★★★

"Why do you think you were attacked tonight?" Gourry asked as we made our way back through the roofed passageway. After what had happened that morning, I dreaded that stupid corridor, but it was the only route from the temple back to the central palace.

"Beats me," I murmured. It still hurt a little to talk, but I knew the pain wouldn't last—those healers were hardcore. "I figured they'd be after Phil. At first, I thought maybe he just snuck into the wrong room, but I'm pretty sure he meant to get to me."

"Hmm," Gourry uttered, thinking. "Maybe . . ."

"Maybe what?"

"Maybe he was just trying to ask you out on a date?"

I groaned. "He's not my type."

"It would help if you laughed at my jokes every once in a while, Lina."

"I'd laugh if they were funny." I sighed and crossed my arms. "Maybe I was just a decoy," I suggested after a moment. "Maybe I was attacked just to divert you and the other guards away from Phil. That way our enemy could get a clear shot at him, right?" I just as quickly refuted my own suggestion in my head; using me as a decoy wouldn't divert that many guards.

"Hmm . . . you know," Gourry said, and I braced myself for another wisecrack.

"Yeah?"

"When you were attacked just now, not one of the guards caught wind of it. Did you notice that?"

I'll be damned. He had a point.

"Why do you think that was?" I asked, intrigued.

Gourry's sensory abilities were superhuman. They were off the charts compared to those of your average guy, so the fact that Gourry'd detected an enemy presence in my room—a presence even I had trouble detecting—came as no real surprise. But the presence (or lack thereof) hadn't caused a stir among the guards protecting Phil, the ones that the enemy would have most wanted to divert. My decoy theory spluttered out like a deflating balloon.

From the passageway, we could see that the guard cover at the palace was every bit as thick as when Gourry and I had snuck in. Zuuma, moreover, had actually killed a number of guards as he'd infiltrated the grounds. But no alarm had gone off. Nothing. He was more invisible than a ghost, it seemed.

But why come for me?

***

"Good morning," I mumbled, bleary-eyed as I greeted Clawfell and Amelia, who were walking across the lawn

toward me. I hoped the stiff black tea I held would wake me up long enough to hold a coherent conversation. After my encounter with Zuuma the night before, I hadn't exactly been able to get back to sleep. A fog hung over my brain, and it felt like pulleys were trying to close my eyes.

After the healing treatment at the temple, Gourry and I had gone back to my room and turned it upside down figuring that there might be something in the room that Zuuma was after, since he had no cause to attack me personally. By sunrise he and I were empty-handed and reduced to a tired heap atop the scattered mess we'd made.

If Zuuma was after something (or someone) in that room, he must've been after whatever (or whoever) it was for a while, because I'd been told it had been vacant for who-knows-how-long before I got there.

"Good morning, Miss Lina!" It was Amelia. I could tell without even turning my head—no one else could possibly sound so bouncy in the morning. "Quite a night, huh?"

You got no idea, missy.

She daintily held a teacup in one hand and waved at me giddily with the other. Amelia was one of those naturally bubbly types, the ones that grate on my nerves within seconds. Luckily for her, I was too tired to be annoyed.

"Let's have a seat," she offered. "You must be exhausted after last night."

Amelia took me by the arm and led me to one of the small tables by the lawn. I was glad to see Clawfell had been released. He sat thoughtfully at our table, pouring aromatic tea into my empty cup.

"Is Gourry with Father?" Amelia asked as my attention wandered.

"Uh, yeah," I replied as I took a sip of my tea. Boy, I was really out of it. At least the tea had a sweet, sharp kick to it that lingered on my tongue and perked up my brain a bit.

Of course, my brain went right back to the exhausting topic of the mission at hand. Just because I got rid of an assassin once didn't mean he wasn't coming back; Zuuma and I would most definitely be seeing each other again. The trick was going to be in capturing him, or anyone in the enemy camp, and getting a solid lead on who was behind all of this.

Sitting out there in the morning was a bit like a stakeout—I needed to keep a vigilant eye on everybody in the Royal Court and whittle down my suspect list gradually.

I didn't much fancy being an assassin's target, but it wasn't like I had any choice in the matter. The best I could hope for now was to dodge whatever they tried next and get to the conspirators before things got really ugly. Since guarding Phil was our primary responsibility, I'd told Gourry to hang close to Phil while I went on scavenging-and-murderer-bait duty alone.

"I wonder why they targeted you," Amelia announced aloud, adding a lump of sugar into the tea that Clawfell had poured her. "It's funny. We were talking with Uncle Christopher about how you were attacked last night, and he looked as surprised as the rest of us."

"Really?" I asked. I thought that if anyone were going to be unfazed by the news, it would have to be Puppet Master Christopher. "And he was for real?"

Amelia shrugged perkily. "That's just it," she said. "It didn't seem like a put-on at all. He just tossed his napkin back on his plate, got up, and walked off in a daze."

I dropped my eyes to my cup, trying to let the information sink in.

Maybe Zuuma's shenanigans had been an impromptu grab for power by a possible rival in Christopher's inner circle. Kanzeil was the only one I could think of at the moment. Whoever it was, it was the first bit of good news I'd had since the fracas had started. It meant that our enemies were disorganized and dogged with some serious leadership issues.

It was time to start poking around at those close to the circle and see what I could dig up. Christopher's son Alfred was as good a start as any—and no, not just because he was moderately hot. I wanted to get a feel for where his loyalties were. Maybe if I finessed him a bit with my feminine charms, I could pry some dirt out of him.

"Let me ask you about Alfred," I said, taking my first shot across the bow. "What's he like?"

Amelia started tracing her finger around an imaginary pattern on the tablecloth. "Well," she said, "why don't ask him yourself?"

"And I can *answer* myself," said a voice behind me. I turned my head to see Alfred standing there like he was a posing for a portrait.

How long had he been there? I bet he could've stood there all day in that debonair way with his cape and his hand at his hip, drinking in the admiring stares of all the royal ladies.

"Where are my manners?" I piped up. "Would you care to join us?"

Alfred smoothed out the folds in his silk shirt, flipped his cape off his shoulder, and strutted toward us. He took a seat at a chair next to mine.

"So, what is it you want to ask me?" he said in his butterscotch voice, nibbling on a grape. Then he stared into a silver tureen sitting at our table and swept several waves of his thick hair back with his fingers. Amelia and I stared at each other, but Alfred was oblivious to our reactions.

Is this guy for real?

There's a simple classification for what Alfred was: a complete and utter narcissist. He's the kind of guy who's all talk and no action, and when things inevitably get nasty he tucks tail and runs, leaving a trail of blame for others. On the flip side, narcissists like Alfred are usually pretty gullible and easy to control.

Okay lesson over.

"Well," I said, "I was curious as to how a sensitive guy like you is taking all the goings-on at the palace."

He took a deep breath and straightened up in his chair. Then he made a point of glancing around the garden before leaning in toward me. "Since you ask," he said with false importance, "I don't like what's going on at all." He brushed a bit of dust from his sleeve. "Even though my father's behind it."

I almost fell out of my chair.

He what now?!

I wasn't sure blurting out a comment like that, whether he meant it or not, was such a good idea given the tense circumstances. I cast my eyes over to Clawfell who was discretely glancing around to make sure no one had overheard. Luckily, there were no eavesdroppers, at least not within earshot.

"Oh, c'mon!" Alfred scoffed. "Anyone with a brain in his head knows my father's behind it all. Am I right?" For someone accusing his own father of conspiring against the king's heir, Alfred sounded awfully nonchalant.

"Believe me," he continued. "I've tried to talk my father out of it several times. But no matter what I say, he always responds with, 'It's for the sake of the kingdom!' " Alfred munched on more grapes. The rest of us just stared dumbly at him. "I think he really does believe he's acting in the best interests of the kingdom and not just for himself. But, you know, I'm not trying to defend what he's doing."

Amelia suddenly got out of her chair and made to leave. Alfred, surprisingly, leapt up and caught her by the arm.

"Amelia, please!" He held onto that arm like his life depended on it. "I came here this morning to ask a favor of you, just this once. I think it would be best if Uncle Phil and my father sat down together and hashed out their differences through dialogue." Amelia didn't respond, just blinked uncomfortably. "Will you help me get them to sit down and talk to each other? I think if Phil explains his position, my father would surely understand!"

Alfred looked intently into Amelia's eyes as he spoke. Don't hold me to it, but he darn well *looked* like he meant what he was saying. Of course, guys like Alfred are also good for putting on a show if it gets them what they want. I wondered if Amelia was thinking the same thing.

She kept her mouth shut tight as she thought. Finally, to my surprise, she said, "All right. I'll try to persuade Father to meet Uncle."

"Wonderful!" exhaled Alfred, like a weight had been lifted off his shoulders. "Thank you, Amelia!" He scooted around the table and hugged her closely. "You talk to your father, and I'll talk to mine. Here's to diplomacy!"

With that, Alfred spun around and dashed off toward the central palace.

Amelia, Clawfell, and I sat rooted to our chairs and watched him go. We exchanged stunned looks, all of us unsure as to whether the clouds were parting and our troubles were ending or if they'd just gotten deeper.

I broke the silence. "So? What do you think of his story, Amelia?"

WHY ME?! WHAT DID I DO?!

She thought a moment. "Well, he sort of put me on the spot." She quickly shook her head, then looked up at me and smiled vaguely. "Either way, the stakes are getting higher."

"But you know," she added, still sporting that same strange smile, "I really don't like that you can't trust people in your own family around here."

It could've been my imagination, but just then I sensed a great sadness in Amelia behind that bubbly façade. There was definitely more to that girl than met the eye.

***

"I am *zonked*." I collapsed into the feather-soft bed in my room. Sighing, I pulled the sheets close to my face and breathed in the sweet scent of Not on My Feet.

Gourry frowned. "Lina," he warned, "you'd better not fall asleep."

"I'm just testing out the goods, pal. Relax." I yawned and stretched, then pulled myself to a sitting position and tried to wake up my brain. I smacked myself across the face a few times—that usually does the trick. Unfortunately, that strategy also tends to freak out those around me, but Gourry was used to it. He just leaned against the nightstand until I was finished.

Gourry and I needed a hardcore powwow to come up with a game plan. All I could think of at the moment was soaking in a warm bath, devouring a gourmet supper, and hitting the sack without any regard for waking up any time soon. But Gourry was right—we had things to hammer out first.

"You know," Gourry said uncomfortably, "you really seem out of it lately."

I yawned. "I know. All this pomp and ceremony kinda throws me off."

Gourry nodded. He still didn't seem too happy.

"I'll say," he muttered.

"So I'm a bit off right now. Is that a problem?" I couldn't help it; I felt a little rattled.

"Since you asked," Gourry replied, "yeah. I've got a *big* problem with it."

I scowled. "Then why didn't you bring this up before?" But Gourry just stared dead ahead at the wall across the room and didn't say a word.

"In case you haven't noticed," I said pointedly, "we're in the Royal Palace. Everybody here's nobility—there's a protocol with that, and we've gotta work around it. It's not like out in the real world where you can confront your enemies toe-to-toe and have it out." I didn't want to be so cross with him, but I had to stand my ground. "We need *subtlety*, Gourry. If I seem a little off, that's just because I'm working with new rules."

Gourry shrugged. "And since when do you follow rules?"

I hopped off the bed. "You're just frustrated right now," I told him. "Now, do you have any new information?"

Gourry shook his head gloomily. "Nope."

"No rumors?" I asked. "No gossip?"

"Not a peep."

I sighed. "Well . . . something *sorta* interesting happened on my end."

I told Gourry about my encounter with Alfred that morning, about how he'd admitted his father's crimes and the solution he'd proposed to Amelia.

"What vibes are you getting from that?" I asked Gourry when I was done.

"Vibes?"

"You know, do you think it's a trap or some kinda act?"

Gourry slowly smirked. "Duh!" he answered. "How can it *not* be a trap?"

Okay, maybe I deserved that, but it was a question worth asking.

"Whether or not it's a trap, I say we go ahead with whatever Alfred's proposing. It may move things along to our advantage. Who knows?"

Gourry raised an eyebrow. "So for lack of a better idea, you just wanna let Alfred control things, hope that Phil doesn't get murdered, and pray everything works itself out in the process?"

It sounded so *sketchy* when he said it. I admit that Gourry had me pegged, but he didn't have to be such a tool about it.

***

The next morning felt like any other at the palace. At first glance, everything looked pretty normal: the guards were at their posts, and the Royal Officers were all going about their daily routine. But if you scratched the surface a little bit, you'd find that a lot had changed since the previous day.

"I wonder what happened with the meeting," I ventured to ask Gourry over lunch in the small dining room. He and I were the only ones around besides the waiter, who seemed so jittery and out-of-sorts that I'm surprised he didn't die of sheer nerves while serving us our squid stew.

"What meeting?" asked Gourry, gulping down his drink and following it with a burp.

I was so stunned for a moment that I dropped my spoon into my soup.

What meeting? How did that guy put his pants on in the morning?!

"You moron!" I gurgled, keeping my voice low so the waiter couldn't hear me. He was having a hard enough time coping as it was. "Did you keep your sausagey fingers jammed in your ears during our talk last night?! The meeting between . . . you know."

Gourry thought for a second. "Oh, that." He went back to his soup. "Why didn't you say so in the first place? You could've been talking about any meeting, Lina."

He's kidding, right?

"What *other* meeting could I have been talking about? Think, Gourry!" I sighed, frustrated. "I don't know exactly what time the two met, but we should've gotten wind of something by now, don't you think?"

I turned my attention to my stew. The spoon I'd dropped into the bowl had completely sunk to the bottom of it and out of sight.

"Great," I snarled. With my fork, I tried to fish the spoon out of the stew. The fork jabbed at something just under the surface of the stew that felt . . . And then, I kid you not, *blood came spurting out of my stew!*

I lurched backward in my chair in total shock. Gourry shot out of his seat, wide-eyed, and we both screamed in unison.

Now, I may not know everything. But I'm pretty sure your lunch projectile bleeding means something is very wrong.

Dozens of long tentacles, streaked purple and brown, came leaping out of the bowl. Gourry and I stumbled to avoid the lashing; we were too dumbfounded to do anything else.

"L-L-Lina!" Gourry shouted. "If this is a prank, it isn't very funny!"

"Do you see me laughing?!" I shot back. "And you know I never order my food this rare!"

The tentacles, unfortunately, just kept getting longer and longer—they could've crushed the entire banquet table in their grasp. What made all this even creepier was the roast chicken: I stopped hollering long enough to notice it suddenly split in half. Gourry and I watched as its belly ripped open and a pair of hands came writhing out from its insides.

I swear, if I'd so much as nibbled on that chicken before witnessing that, I would've hunted that chef down and roasted him on a spit myself. If there's one thing I hate more than lousy food and lousy service, it's a chef who puts nightmarish monsters in my order.

The tentacled stew-creature emerging from my bowl plopped onto the table. I can't describe its body any better than to compare it to a large, rubbery ball with dozens of gnarled tentacles that looked like shiny, slithery tree roots. And, what looked like a deformed humanoid, was emerging from the chicken. That's what I said—a deformed humanoid emerged from my chicken, except this creature was swathed in seaweed.

"I-I swear I didn't order that!" Gourry stammered.

"I believe you!" I shouted. "Now RUN!"

When in doubt: run. It was the only strategy that came to mind. I darted for the nearest door and swung it open, but froze when I saw what lay beyond it. Gourry crashed into my back and nearly knocked me over.

The room on the other side looked weirdly familiar. I saw a banquet table laden with exotic foods, made far less appetizing by a jungle of writhing tentacles and a seaweed monster. Identical copies of Gourry and me stood right in front of us, framed in the doorway and staring like a pair of slack-jawed idiots.

A mirror spell. "Gourry!" I exclaimed. "Do you realize what this means?"

"What?!"

I waved to my own reflection, then smiled dumbly as it waved and smiled dumbly back. "Cool," we murmured.

Sorry—couldn't help it

"Cut it out!" Gourry snapped, slamming the door shut. He looked down at me urgently. "What the hell was that all about?"

"A mirroring spell," I replied. "You don't see *that* everyday."

"What kinda wizard could cast a spell like that?!"

I shook my head. "We're definitely trapped here by whoever's doing the casting, though. I don't think we have a choice." I smirked at him. "You ready to fight those creepy-crawly things?"

Gourry took a deep, firm breath and nodded. I began chanting a spell as he drew his sword and advanced toward the now-moving body of the tentacled creature. He took rapid, sweeping swipes with his blade to hack past the tentacles, then lunged for the body with a yell.

Squelch!

His sword made a squishy slide deep inside the Stew Monster Ball. Unfortunately, the thing didn't die—and it definitely got madder.

"What . . . the hell?" Gourry spluttered.

"Keep at it!" I yelled.

Gourry kept wildly slashing at the creature. "Easy to say from over there!" he shot back. He seemed a bit panicky, and I guess I would've been too with all those tentacles trying to wrap themselves around me. I noticed more tentacles snaking around the table toward his legs, while other tentacles rose higher and spewed clods of what looked like black mud at him.

"Look out!" I screamed, but Gourry was already on it. He hacked at those slithery devils before they had a chance to retreat.

A bunch of black globs spattered the walls and floor. I had no idea how deadly they might be to bare human skin, but even my sorceress curiosity didn't compel me to find out. Deadly potions and poisons kinda do it for me, but not when I'm inches away from being killed by them.

Just as I was about to yell at Gourry, a flat, squirmy guest began emerging from the tureen on the banquet.

Enough is enough—we don't have all day!

"Gourry!" I called. "Use the Sword of Light!"

Gourry sheathed his sword. "Gotcha!" he called back as he fished a needle from a pocket. He maneuvered it into his hilt to release the blade, pulled out his empty grip, and brandished it two-handed. "Light come forth!"

A beam of brilliant white light burst forth to form his blade.

One day, baby . . . you will be mine, the sword that is.

In case you've been living in a cave with your fingers in your ears, Gourry was holding the one-and-only Sword of Light. By focusing the energy and spirit of its wielder, the Sword can cleave a demon in half like a machete through a ripe banana.

When the tentacles sensed the Sword's presence, they actually quivered in fear before frantically flinging more clods at Gourry. With lightning reflexes, Gourry dodged the muddy missiles, wove through the tentacles, and plunged the light beam directly through Seaweed Man.

I wasn't surprised to see the creature wither and his body turn to dry earth. With a dull thud, Mr. Ocean Vegetation fell to a pile on the floor and immediately began to vaporize into thin air.

Lest you get the impression I was just the bystander—you know, some sort of damsel-in-distress—let me turn your attention to my marvelous feats of magic. Gourry had dealt with the onslaught of tentacles and Seaweed Man, so

I decided to throw my focus on the new manta-ray-thing wriggling its way down the dinner table.

"Elmekia Lance!" My spell blasted a nasty hole through its floppy back. It was just as I suspected: our attackers, apparently, had originated in the astral plane—the place where physical form doesn't exist. The spell I used inflicts damage directly to an opponent's mind, bypassing the body entirely. In other words, the blasted-out hole told me the monster was spiritual rather than physical. That's some heavy stuff, huh?

Regardless, the important thing was that Mr. Ocean Vegetation was dead. Just like Seaweed Man, the manta ray deteriorated within seconds and crumbled to the floor. I wasn't finished yet. I was still sore about my lunch being ruined by some jerkoff, so I drew my sword and struck the criminal tureen. The stew had turned into a stinky, bubbly broth that now cooled into greenish goo.

Um . . . yuck.

I also cleaved the split-open roast chicken, just to make sure no other tricks were hiding inside it.

Okay, destroying crockery with my sword was probably no great act of courage, but it still felt pretty damn good.

It didn't *look* like the kitchenware or chicken were spiritual *or* any more of a threat, so I turned to Gourry who was still having trouble with the giant tomato and its crap-flinging tentacles.

"What are you doing?!" I yelled.

"Losing!" Gourry cried. "This guy won't die!"

Hmph. An overgrown bouncy ball was no match for Lina Inverse! I quickly began chanting a spell. Both Black Magic and astral spells can inflict damage directly to an attacker's spirit, but they do little good if the spells themselves aren't powerful enough. I braced myself and hoped for the best.

The tomato bounced around Gourry's light blade, thrashed its tentacles, and volleyed yet another black mass straight at me.

I barely managed to dodge the goop as I hit the floor hard, knocking over the table and bringing it with me to use as a shield.

So the tomato wants to play dirty, eh? Two can play that game!

"Dark Claw!" I yelled.

I lunged from behind the table, twisting my body and firing a shot toward the fray that surrounded Gourry. The shapeless magic blast whooshed toward the monster ball, but that little creep just danced out of the way. Unfortunately, that left Gourry in the path of my magic.

"Hey!" he shouted, just barely swatting the missile off with his Sword of Light. I don't know if it was a lucky shot or an example of his brilliant swordsmanship, but Gourry actually batted the missile straight into the creature. That fat sucker and its infuriating tentacles crumbled into dust before it knew what hit 'em.

Gourry and I glanced at each other as we tried to catch our breath. Our battle with our lunch was finally over.

"Whew!" I wiped some sweat from my brow and smiled. "No one can get past our one-two punch, eh, Gourry?" I raised two fingers to flash a V-for-Victory sign.

"What one-two punch?" Gourry panted, an alarmed look on his face. "What were you trying to do? Cook me alive?!"

"Now, now," I cooed. "We won, and that's what counts."

Gourry was apparently too tired to retort. He just slumped into his chair, exhausted, and still rattled.

"Of all the things I thought would kill me," he murmured, "I never guessed you or a mutant octopus tomato."

I upturned my chair from the floor and sat down beside him. "At least we can relax now," I told him. "And I think we worked off lunch."

After sitting in silence for a minute, the waiter stepped in through the door that led to the kitchen.

"Excuse me," he said, looking us over with concern. "Is everything all right?"

Gourry and I suddenly noticed that everything in the room was back to normal. The banquet table was perfectly set with the tureen of stew, the plate of roast chicken, the fancy crockery, and the expensive silverware all in their proper places.

Only one detail was different: my mantle. The various blasts I'd released during the fight had done a number on it, leaving it tattered and scorched.

Crap, I just bought that mantle.

"All right?" Gourry asked blankly.

"Gourry," I interrupted, then shook my head to keep him from saying anything else. I leaned closer and whispered to him, "He obviously has no clue as to what just happened. It's like real-world time stopped during our food fight."

The waiter still stood in the doorway, rooted to the ground and obviously confused. Gourry proved faster-than-normal on the uptake, since a second later he turned to the waiter and shook his head solemnly.

"If you don't mind," he murmured, "we'd like to skip the stew course."

I gasped and turned to him in shock. "Are you *nuts?!*" I cried. "It'll take more than that to scare me off squid stew!"

***

"I-I can't believe this has happened," Alfred whimpered, sliding weakly into an oversized chair.

Amelia, Phil, Alfred, Gourry and I had gathered in a guesthouse adjacent to the central palace. The room was as big as a barn, but by Saillune terms it was downright intimate, and since guards stood just outside the door, we felt safe enough for a secret meeting.

"I only found out about the attack on Miss Lina and Mr. Gourry this afternoon," Alfred said grimly. He ran his trembling fingers through his perfect hair. "What an absolutely dreadful ordeal."

Us fighting stew, or Mr. Pansy hearing the scary report?

"Mmm," Phil grunted, scowling and folding his arms. "What the hell is Chris thinking?!"

"I don't think my father is behind this, Uncle." Alfred shook his head. "I can't see him as the perpetrator."

"Young man," Phil said, "protecting your father right now is only going to make our investigation more difficult."

Alfred clasped his hands together in a plea. "Please," he begged. "I know you'll find it hard to believe, Uncle, but my father was *shocked* when I told him the news. I'm certain he knew nothing about this!"

"Of course he didn't," I muttered under my breath. I didn't think anyone had heard me, but Phil perked up and leaned in my direction.

"And just what do you mean by that?" he questioned.

I let out a breath and sat up. "Well," I explained, "the way things stand right now, Chris has nothing to gain by attacking Gourry and me. Going after us would draw even more suspicion to himself, right?"

The others nodded in agreement, though a bit grudgingly. We were still no closer to an answer.

"So if it wasn't Chris," I wondered aloud, "who was it?"

Alfred suddenly jumped to his feet, snapping his fingers. "It's Kanzeil running amok!"

You stole the words right out of my mouth.

"After I told my father what happened," he said, "Father looked at me like he'd just seen a ghost. Then he immediately sent one of his servants to fetch Kanzeil—it was the first thing out of his mouth." He nodded to himself. "Kanzeil *has* to be behind this."

Then, in a sudden moment of overgrown immaturity, Alfred huffed and stomped his boots on the floor. "Dammit!" he whined. "I should've known from the beginning he was no good!" Alfred slammed both fists on the table and buried his face in his hands, further proving that he tantrumed like a toddler.

"Who is this Kanzeil fellow, anyway?" It was Amelia's turn to speak up. "I mean, where's he from, and what does he want?"

"I haven't the faintest," Alfred groaned. "One morning Kanzeil came to the palace accompanying Father, and by lunch he'd become my father's advisor. I tried to ask about the man, but all Father would tell me was that Kanzeil was an old acquaintance and that he knew nothing of where he was from."

"I don't care about his background," Phil snapped. "I just want him out of all matters of the Royal Court. Is that understood?"

At that, Amelia, Gourry, and I chimed in at once, running over each other's words.

"What do you mean?" Alfred asked impatiently over all of us. It was the last thing I heard before an ominous silence fell over the room and I no longer sensed the guards outside.

Their presence had been replaced with a keen and ferocious bloodlust that now lurked just behind the locked door.

"Assassins," I whispered, and I cast a quick glance at Gourry. He gripped the hilt of his sword and nodded that he was ready to face the threat.

I turned back to the door and tried to focus my senses on the enemy. I felt several of them outside, and all of them deadly. If they'd wiped out Phil's five bodyguards without letting out a peep, this was not going to be a picnic.

Of course, it made way more sense if the enemy had Zuuma; that guy could kill the average guard without getting out of bed. Wracking my brain fervently for ideas, I wondered if we could sound an alarm to the guards in the central palace. It would reinforce our numbers and give us a better shot at survival . . . but then I remembered all the nearby guards were dead, and our room was sound-proofed to protect our secret meeting.

Our *not*-so-secret meeting, apparently.

Since our room had no windows and only a tiny ventilation shaft, the door was the only means of entry and escape. I didn't fancy using that door—since an ambush was definitely waiting outside—so we had no choice but to hold our ground and brace for a fight.

"We either fight them here," Gourry thought aloud, "or we figure a way to break out of this place."

Break out? Of course!

"Gourry!" I grabbed his sleeve. "Let's push the table up against the door and barricade ourselves!"

A strategy was forming in my nimble brain.

"Barricade?" Gourry looked down at me, surprised. "But that'll trap us in here like rats!"

"Trust me," I said. "It'll buy us time. Now get to it!"

I guess he knew better than to ask at that point, so he grabbed the table and dragged it to the door. I turned to Amelia and, pointing to the wall opposite the door, asked, "Is there a courtyard on the other side of this wall?"

Amelia nodded, breathing deeply and staying remarkably calm. She definitely took after her father in that respect. Phil had a tendency to stay very poised in times of crises. I tapped the wall a few times with my fingers to test its thickness.

I finally stepped back. "Okay!" I announced to the room. "Everybody stand back, because I'm gonna blow this mother up!"

I heard Alfred shriek girlishly and the others scamper away while I began to chant. On the other side of the room, Gourry and Phil finished barricading the door.

I completed my chant and pressed both hands against the wall. "Blast Wave!" I yelled, and the power of my magic blew outward full force.

KA-BOOM!

A huge circular portion of the wall exploded, sending pumpkin-sized chunks of debris out into the courtyard and creating a hole big enough for us to escape through.

"This way!" I called to the others.

Trying not to choke too badly on the dust from the blast, I led the way through the hole and over the debris-peppered ground. The enemy's presence suddenly reared up above me, his bloodlust raging like a pissed-off dragon.

"Damn!" I snarled, and instinctively leapt to one side. It's a good thing I did—a split-second later, something metallic shot through the air and buried itself deep in the ground where I'd been standing.

A dark figure standing on the roof flashed a single dagger about the length of an outstretched hand and leapt into the air straight for Gourry.

"You're mine!" Gourry cried and swung his sword so swiftly that he could've made two of anyone stupid enough to be within reach. Unfortunately, Gourry's sword only slashed through thin air; the assassin had halted his dive midair and confused the dickens out of Gourry. Then, banking on Gourry's brief confusion, the assassin attempted a floating scissor-kick at Gourry.

Nice Try!

"Flare Arrow!" I commanded as fast as I could, launching a dozen of them, several of which scored a direct hit and sent the assassin plummeting to the ground, tumbling into a pile of rubble.

Ah . . . it's good to be me!

While I was dispatching our levitating friend; Phil, Amelia, and Alfred had finished scrambling into the courtyard. A slew of guards rushed toward us. If the explosion hadn't caught their attention, I figured my light show might've.

BOOM!

An explosion from inside the room splintered the door and hurled the oak table out of the way. Just as two silhouettes appeared in the destroyed doorway, four silver daggers shot from their direction and tore through the air toward Phil.

"Look out!" I yelled.

As I did, Amelia deftly swiped her mantle. There was a flash of white light before three of the daggers went clattering to the ground. Phil caught the fourth dagger with his bare hand, and then dropped it without ceremony.

"HOLY CRAP!" the assassins yelled in unison.

They were as shocked as Gourry and I. It's one thing to get out of the way of whatever's attacking you, but to beat your attacker at their own game is something entirely different—an impressive showing from the father-daughter duo. And from the looks of it, Amelia wasn't through.

"Fools!" she roared, pointing an angry finger at the assassins. "You have turned your backs against heavenly truth by sullying your hands with evil! Watch your instruments of destruction break before my Justice!" "Break before my Justice?"

Amelia had definitely dreamed of this heroic moment all her life. There she stood, fiery and defiant, and about 140 percent more dramatic than she needed to be.

But in a surprising moment of epic glory, she actually began rising into the air. Then I noticed what—or should I say, who—was keeping her up so high. Phil had grabbed her by the back of her mantle and lifted her like a kitten.

"Stand aside, Amelia," he boomed. "This is no place for a little girl."

Phil then tossed her in our direction. Amelia landed gracefully, not once faltering in her fearless dignity.

"Be a good little princess and take your own advice!" one of the assassins shrieked. He rushed from his side of the room and charged right for Phil, who squared his shoulders and prepared to lock horns.

For our part, Gourry and I stayed on Phil's heels, prepared to brace against whatever onslaught was about to take place.

"Foooooools!" Phil roared imperiously and swung his tightly clenched fist at the assassin.

POW!

The poor assassin practically bounced off Phil's fist and went flying into the wall. He hit it with a crunch, then, like flung fudge, slid down to the floor in a gooey little heap.

"I know not why you support this conspiracy!" Phil boomed, stepping toward his attacker. He then launched into a long, solemn speech, which wasn't inherently bad—except for the fact that the guy was already dead, judging by the rather severe angle at which his neck was bent.

"Have you no family?!" Phil demanded of the corpse. "Open your eyes!"

Uh . . . that ain't happenin', Phil.

"Morally abasing yourselves in this manner brings your family nothing but grief and shame! I care not for unnecessary violence." He pointed to the other assassins. "If you look into your own hearts and reflect, and leave this place at once, I shall hold no grudge against you!"

That was when the other assassins ran over to check their dead partner. One of them felt for a pulse; the others mumbled among themselves, and all of them glanced at Phil.

They ran. I thought I saw one look back, but that may have just been a trick of the light.

"Then no grudge shall it be." Phil sighed heavily, shaking his head in true jaded-warrior fashion. "I wish only that you all see the errors of your way and spare your loved ones further torment."

From a short distance away came the clip-clop of soldiers' boots heading in our direction. *About time*, I thought, finally sliding my hand off my sword hilt. I didn't blame Phil for keeping Gourry and me so close all the time—his own guards weren't exactly *useful*.

Gourry gently prodded the dead assassin with his foot. "Man," he commented with a low whistle. "Looks like we scraped through again. But we're safe now!"

First rule of jinxes: never, *ever* say that.

Danger filled every one of my senses so fast that it nearly knocked me over. All I could do was scream, "GET DOWN!"

We'd barely hit the dirt when a giant explosion went off in the room.

KA-BOOM!

I threw my arms over my head to protect it from the tiny bits of rubble that flew in our direction. In the few seconds of immediate calm after the blast, I heard chunks of something soft and wet splatter down on what little remained of the room.

Chunks?

You know, it'd been a long enough night without me having to guess what would go *splat* after an explosion. After a quick swallow to make sure my stomach contents were firmly down, I tentatively raised my head and squinted my eyes in the direction of the room.

The dead assassin had been blown apart. Charred flesh, buckets of blood, and what were probably bits of organs were splattered all over the rubble of the room. It was pretty gruesome—not a sight, nor a smell for that matter, you'd want to cap off your day with.

"What happened?!" a guard yelled frantically.

"Are you safe, my lord?" another called.

Dozens of guards rushed in from all corners of the courtyard, clattering their spears and swords with purpose and in general looking like they thought they were making a difference.

Thanks for showing up for the afterparty, guys.

I slowly got to my feet, glad we'd all survived with only minor cuts and bruises. The guards ran to Phil and tried to check him for wounds, but the prince brushed them off to survey the damage.

Mmm . . ." he murmured, looking gravely at the wreckage all around him. He shook his head. "In all my years," he said at last, "no one has ever been so moved by my words, so aggrieved by their evil deeds that they exploded out of sheer shame." He lowered his eyes and seemed deeply upset.

Yeah, I'm not even gonna touch that one.

Phil's nonsensical blabbering did get me thinking, though. Why had the other assassins felt the need to check the dead guy's pulse? Lemme tell you . . . when a man's neck is snapped and half of the bones in his body are shattered, you don't need the pulse-check. That's what we call using *context clues*.

My hunch was that the whole checking-up-on-their-comrade routine had just been an act. They must've done it to plant an explosive device on the dead man, simultaneously baiting our humanitarian sensibilities and hoping we'd check the guy again after they left—thus getting us, of course, blown to kingdom come.

"Excellency!" one guard hollered. "What happened?!"

"We were assaulted by petty knaves," Phil replied, shrugging his shoulders. "Don't be concerned; we're all safe now."

"Knaves, you say?!" The men huffed angrily. The incident had definitely worked them up; they anxiously shuffled around, waiting for orders.

Then their captain—the same guy we'd come across the day we arrived at the palace—started barking out orders: "Squad 1 and Squad 2, remain here! Squad 3, search the building! Squad 4, search the surrounding area! If you find any of those knaves, capture them and bring them back alive! You, contact the central palace . . ." He went on like that for a while, but I was too dazed after what had just happened to really follow what the guards were up to.

They could search the grounds all they wanted—they weren't going to find anybody. I was sure the assassins were already long gone.

"You know," I mumbled to Gourry as we watched the guards disperse, "something's bothering me. Is it just me, or did Zuuma not show up for a piece of the action this time?"

Gourry nodded. Apparently he was thinking the exact same thing. Unfortunately, a piercing cry suddenly tore through the air and startled any remaining thoughts right out of my brain.

"Why?!" It was Alfred, throwing another baby fit. He was beginning to wear on me. Judging from his harried look and the demented gleam in his eyes, I thought Alfred was just inches away from a mental breakdown. Still, I tried to follow what he was getting at.

"Th-Th-The attack today!" he stammered, "Could that have been for . . . ?

"Could that have been for *what*?" Phil asked sharply.

Alfred didn't respond—he just kept trembling, his fingers fidgeting and his eyes roving among us. Then he suddenly cried, "Father! I must check on Father!" And with that, he took off toward the central palace, tripping over several hedges and a guard helmet along the way.

Phil watched him disappear into the night. The prince threw me a look. "What was that all about?"

I began to answer, but then stopped short. There was too good a chance we'd be overheard out there in the open. "We can't discuss it outside," I whispered to Phil as I scanned the grounds for loitering guards.

"Indeed," agreed Phil. He gestured for Gourry, Amelia, and me to proceed to the palace.

"All I'll say for now," I told him, "is that I think this is a lot more complicated than any of us had guessed."

Phil nodded shortly.

***

In the central palace, Phil set up an impromptu meeting in his personal quarters. Maybe it wasn't the ideal place for a powwow—we still had to speak in hushed tones because there were guards outside—but it sure beat the alternative. I definitely preferred Phil's cushy chairs and decent lighting to the blown-out room splattered with assassin meat.

Phil took a deep breath. "All right," he said carefully. "Let's start from the beginning." He furrowed his bushy eyebrows. "Alfred said earlier that he thought Kanzeil attacked you at lunch. Does that theory still hold water?"

I crossed my arms. "Maybe," I replied after a moment.

"Attacking us at lunch wouldn't have benefited Christopher. An attack that conspicuous leaves people wondering, and since half the palace already thinks he's up to no good, it could only make him look worse." I gripped my chin. "But . . . hmm."

"Something wrong, Lina?" Gourry asked.

I frowned. "Bear with me for a sec. Whoever sent the monsters probably would've known we'd find the attack uncharacteristic of Christopher. And then if Christopher looked shocked and summoned Kanzeil in front of Alfred, and then Alfred ran to us and set a meeting to discuss it . . ."

Amelia clenched her fists. "He knew we'd all be in one place tonight. It was the perfect time to move in for the kill!"

"Exactly," I replied. "I don't think the attack at lunch was supposed to succeed—I think it was just supposed to get us all together tonight. Christopher could've ordered that attack at lunch and then faked the whole surprise to throw off Alfred."

Phil stomped one massive foot. "Unforgivable!" he roared, far too loudly for a secret meeting. "Such treacherousness is too much to bear! The thought of him gathering us in one place and recklessly putting his son in harm's way? This has gone too far!"

"Hang on," I piped in, trying to calm him down. "That's just one theory, all right? Christopher may have nothing to do with it."

Phil fumed. "After all he's already done?! I'm no longer giving that man the benefit of the doubt!"

"Listen," I said as calmly as I could. "Just because Christopher *could've* been behind tonight doesn't mean he *was*. Besides putting Alfred at risk, let's not forget why we suspected Kanzeil in the first place—Christopher's already-slipping reputation. Kanzeil could've easily sent the demons and guessed Alfred's train of thought, so he could've done this whole elaborate scheme behind Christopher's back."

Phil went silent for a moment, I breathed a little sigh of relief; at least mulling over options kept him from yelling.

"So, tell me." Phil threw a burning gaze in my direction. "What do you *honestly* think?"

"Honestly?" I repeated. "I think today was all Kanzeil." I frowned. "But there's one piece that still doesn't fit."

"And what is that?"

"The fact that tonight's attack failed. Us being together was a carefully planned window of opportunity, yet the assassins weren't particularly impressive and eventually chose to retreat. Zuuma was way more hardcore when he tried to—"

Amelia gasped. "Wait a sec!" she cried. "D-did you just say Zuuma?"

I blinked. Amelia's eyes were as wide as dinner plates, and she'd risen from her chair.

Why, do I have a bad feeling about this?

"Um, yeah," I answered slowly. "He attacked me the other night."

She gasped again. "Really?!"

"Really."

"So, he *is* real," she muttered. She was beginning to give me the creeps.

"You've heard of this man?" Phil ventured to ask.

Amelia nodded vigorously. "He's supposed to be one of the deadliest assassins out there. I'm so glad you're okay, Miss Lina! If the rumors are true, that would make you the first person to ever survive his pursuit!"

My stomach dropped like a stone sailboat. *Ever?* I repeated silently as my mind and belly reeled. I realized that if Gourry hadn't shown up that night, I would've ended up as just another notch on that celebrity killer's belt.

Note to self: thank Gourry again for breaking down my door.

If there was any consolation here, it was a teeny-tiny one. "At least Zuuma wasn't part of the attack tonight," I murmured. "Maybe that means something, and maybe it doesn't. Zuuma could've just run out of time to prepare an attack, for all we know."

Phil thwacked his leg with one hand. "Enough of this," he snapped. "The only way to resolve this is through face-to-face dialogue. I'll have that meeting with Christopher tomorrow and put an end to all this nonsense!"

Somehow I doubted words were going to fix much of anything. But Phil needed something to believe in, so I kept my mouth shut and let him hope.

***

On the morning of Phil and Christopher's big conference, the entire palace brimmed with nervous excitement.

Alfred had apparently gone to see his father and Kanzeil the evening of the guesthouse attack. Both Christopher and Kanzeil had denied involvement, but what else had Alfred expected? "Sure, we tried to murder you and the royal heir in one clever fatal swoop. But here, have a cookie!" *Duh.*

Eldoran, the reigning and ailing king, was living in denial. No matter how much you pressed the issue with him, Eldoran refused to believe that Christopher could possibly be plotting to usurp Phil's inheritance to the throne. As far as he was concerned, his two sons skipped along as sweet and loyal brothers. Maybe Eldoran believing in that crap was the only thing keeping him alive. That, or the anxiety of the future of the throne, had been what sent him to his sickbed in the first place.

Whatever the case, that day's conference was crucial for the future well-being of Eldoran's kingdom. If things fell apart, Gourry and I didn't relish the idea of having to put the pieces back together.

Gourry, Amelia, Alfred, Kanzeil, and I all followed Christopher and Phil as they made their way out of the central palace. Something told me we'd be seeing Zuuma before the day was out, and I doubted it would be for a friendly chat and tea. At least it was a nice day: bright sunshine greeted us as we descended the palace's front steps, and the garden was bedecked with flowers of the most amazing colors.

In direct contrast with the weather, Kanzeil turned toward me and cracked the iciest smile I'd ever seen. It took all my willpower to not slap that ridiculous grin off his conniving little face.

As we walked, I leaned over to Gourry and muttered, "About Kanzeil . . ."

Gourry seemed to have noticed Kanzeil's smile. He nodded. "Yeah?"

"I think he's coming on to me."

Gourry gave a short, pained laughed. "You've got some guts, cracking jokes at a time like this."

I shrugged. "I could use a laugh these days." Gourry leaned in a little closer. "Uh, Lina," he whispered, "what if what's-his-face, that assassin fellow, shows up again?" I assumed he meant Zuuma.

"He's all yours," I answered with a brush of my hand.

To this day I don't know if Gourry took what I said seriously. He just straightened, nodded, and answered, "Okay."

Since Gourry had brought up the subject of evil, magic-using assassins, I starting wondering if Kanzeil would try to pull that curved-space trick on me again.

Easy, Lina. Don't panic—just keep your ears open and your eyes peeled.

We made our way to the meeting hall and then watched as Phil and Christopher entered alone. Their private conference was to be held inside. The rest of us waited outdoors, along with the princes' guards, and prepared ourselves for a long round of Power Waiting.

As we sat there, I kept as vigilant a watch as I could on Kanzeil. If he started chanting some spell, I wanted to try and stave it off, but he just hung around and didn't try to murder me once. The morning passed pretty uneventfully, until about halfway through the time allotted for the meeting.

A sound ripped through the air.

ZZZZZZING!

It's hard to explain, but it was as if space itself had suddenly screamed.

"What the hell was that?!" one of the guards yelled. Suddenly, something eclipsed the sunlight, and everything became shrouded in shadow.

I jumped to my feet. *What now?!* I thought as I frantically looked around.

"Lina!" Gourry shouted, pointing upward. "Up there!" He was referring to a massive, black object directly over us and falling fast.

I knew today would suck.

"LOOK OUT!" I yelled at the top of my lungs.

We all scattered like a bunch of panicky ants. When the object hit, it slammed to the ground with such force that it rocked the foundation of the meeting hall. I stumbled to stay on my feet just as the giant projectile screeched.

Giiiiiiiiii! The vibrations in the air rang in my ears and shuddered through my body; I turned to see what in hell could be making such a noise. And there it sat: the largest, freakiest looking beetle I'd ever seen.

Okay, second largest.

When I say it was big, it was *big*. The bug was the size of a small dragon, with an ebony hide, eight hideous legs, and a pair of sinewy wings that were too small for flight but big enough for me to jump onto and go for a ride. What looked like rubies were embedded throughout the beetle's body, and when the stones caught the light, the insect glittered like some kind of grotesque amulet.

I'll admit—it was a creative way to get the battle started.

The guards totally lost it. As panic took over, the lot of them actually tried to mount some kind of resistance against the giant, ugly invader. The problem was that their technique was a mess—a pell-mell of hastily thrown blades and panic-stricken shouts, and none of it proved very effective against our unwelcome guest.

I sincerely doubted the guards *could* do much against that thing. Their spears bounced off the bug's outer shell, and even driving swords into the beetle's leg joints proved a waste of time. In fact, the beetle didn't take much notice of the guards. It rotated on its feet, slowly and heedlessly, and faced what it was looking for.

Me.

3 : SAILLUNE: CAUGHT IN THE FAMILY FEUD

"Wh-what the hell?!" was all I managed to get out. The insect from hell raised its ugly wings. Pointedly facing me in the noisy crowd, the beetle fluttered those wings with a great deal of power.

WHOOSH!

Maybe those wings weren't good for flight, but they sure made for a mighty wind—er—blast.

I remember hurtling for I don't know how long or how far, then rolling across the lawn like a carelessly tossed rag doll.

"O-ow," I wheezed. I lay there, my eyes half-closed, and tried to breathe. Getting the wind knocked out of me had never hurt so *bad*.

"Lina!"

I couldn't tell where the cry came from. Out of the corner of my eye, I caught a glimpse of Kanzeil; in the midst of all the chaos, he just stood there with folded arms. He stared at me, his eyes glittering with explicit malice.

"Lina!"

It was Gourry. I looked back to see him drive his sword through one of the beetle's feet. Nothing.

"Wha?!" Gourry lurched backward, away from the creature. "Now what?!"

Normal weapons obviously had no effect on the thing. This was one nasty demon beast, probably vicious enough to give Zanaffar of Sairaag a run for his money.

But I wasn't about to waste the time Gourry had bought me. I stumbled to my feet; the spell I was chanting was done by the time I stood.

"Atscha Dist!" I roared.

Giiiiiii! The beetle shrieked so loudly that its body quaked and the entire courtyard shuddered with the sound. Apparently, pissing the demon off was the extent of my success.

Dammit! I've used that spell to vaporize vampires, but all it did here was tickle that bug's feet.

The beetle pivoted toward me again and gaped. Without another thought, I flung myself sideways just as the demon sounded off a terrible screech.

A giant, destructive explosion went off several yards behind me. Whipping my head in its direction, I saw the courtyard—the portion of it I'd been standing in, anyway—completely flattened. All greenery had dissipated and the area had turned into a smoking crater.

Hot damn!

Only a shockwave could've caused that damage—a shockwave emitted by the creature itself.

We still had one glint of hope. "Gourry!" I shouted. "Light!"

"Good idea!"

As Gourry worked to unleash his sword, I started chanting another spell. Unfortunately, with soldiers still hacking at the bug, I had to keep the big guns stowed away or run the risk of killing Phil's men. It wasn't exactly a handicap I needed at the moment.

But before I could finish what I was chanting, the beetle swung a leg at me. "Gaa!" I cried as another shockwave slammed me right in the knees. That miserable bastard could send those things with his legs?! The vibration flipped me over and sent me flying backward and upside down.

If I live through this, I'm stomping every beetle I ever see for the rest of my life!

I crashed on the other side of the lawn, reeling and dazed. The good news was that I wasn't dead—I only felt like I was. Grunting and gasping, I stumbled to my feet but then collapsed instantly.

From somewhere in the upheaval, I heard Gourry yell my name. He was nearby, but I was too dazed to even know which way was up.

"What's the meaning of this, Kanzeil!" cried Alfred. "This wasn't part of the plan!"

Good luck, I thought. Talking to that maniac sorcerer had done *so much* already. Blinking pain from my eyes, I fought my head up and turned to the bug.

A swirling beam of plasma appeared between the beetle's antennae. As it arced between the feelers, igniting as it swirled, the blood ran cold in my veins.

A lightning attack?!

It hit me before I could even scream. Be it a blessing or a curse, the magical shock that raced through my body knocked me out before I could register much pain. When I

jolted awake seconds later, I wheezed, fighting to breathe, and looked up to see the bottom of a massive beetle foot . . .

The bug wanted to *squash* me.

I'll admit, the irony hurt. It hurt almost as much as being tossed around all morning like a rejected toy. I could almost hear the town crier the next morning: "Lina Inverse, world-famous sorceress, crushed to death by an insect!" That was *not* acceptable.

Panic shot up my spine as the bug's leg came rushing down to kill me. I could only think one thing:

I don't wanna die a gag!

CHOOM!

A white light streaked across my vision. Whatever it was knocked the demon's leg off-balance, and the foot instead came slamming down in the charred grass by my side. Barely believing I was still breathing, I looked up with wide eyes.

Amelia. She was running toward me, shouting something I couldn't hear. Dazed, I also noticed Gourry, charging toward the off-balance bug with his Sword of Light held high. With a war cry that rang through the air, Gourry hewed off the creature's head as easy as slicing a piece of bug-pie.

Soon after a whole lot of goopy bug-pie filling oozed out, I lost consciousness.

***

"We're quitting this job and getting out of here."

I moaned. *Who said that?*

When I opened my eyes, Gourry was leaning over me. I stared at him a second, then slowly came to the realization that I was in a bed and my heart was still beating.

Gourry must've caught the dazed and puzzled look on my face because he backed away and let me get my bearings. I must've looked a real mess—I tried to brush back my hair and smooth out my sleep-worn face with my hands. Fighting to sit up, I cast my bleary eyes around the room.

It was a spacious place with tidy white walls. I heard a fire crackling in the hearth and the scent of herbs filled the air around me. At the foot of the bed, I noticed a team of concerned magic healers. A few seconds more and I realized I was back in the temple infirmary—the place where Gourry had taken me after my windpipe-crushing encounter with Zuuma. I figured I was quickly becoming the most popular patient at the palace.

Engraved within the floor's stone tiles was a large hexagram. My bed lay exactly in the center of it. "Hey!" Amelia chirped from Gourry's side. "How're you doing?"

"Pretty tired," was all I could muster. "But I can move and nothing hurts too bad." I tried to shift my legs a little under the blankets, but didn't really succeed.

Amelia smiled cheerfully. "Well, that's what happens. But it sure beats the alternative!"

I furrowed my eyebrows. " 'That's what happens?' " I repeated.

"What the hell happened to me out there?"

Gourry averted his eyes. "Uh," he mumbled, "I think it's better if you don't ask."

I raised an eyebrow at Amelia. She just smiled and waved a hand at me.

"Oh, it's nothing to get upset over," she said with inappropriate chipperness. "Your legs got slashed and you have burns all over your body. Nothing *really* major."

Okay. I wasn't ready for that.

"But . . . how?" I asked. "What happened?" I was still trying to wrap my head around the big-bug battle.

"The short end of it is: Mr. Gourry killed the bug with the Sword of Light right before it sliced you up. It was very impressive." She gave him a big smile, further proving she never got tired of doing that to people. "Though I never expected him to have the Sword of Light. How very exciting!"

Great, but I already knew that.

"So you guys killed the thing, then what? Did—"

"Let's not go there," Gourry interrupted. "It doesn't matter, Lina—we're getting out of this mess as of now."

"What? Why?"

"Why?" Gourry repeated, his voice rising in pitch. "Don't you get it, Lina?! It's you they're after. So don't come cryin' to me if your head gets hacked off by one of your many enemies.

Don't worry. I don't think my hacked-off head's gonna do much crying.

I rolled my eyes. "I'm well aware that someone's out to get me," I responded. "Hello context clues."

Sheesh, he didn't have to get so worked up.

"Yeah! So?"

"So, I still have no idea *why* I'm a target. What do you think?"

Gourry blinked. "Uh, I dunno," he said blankly. "What're you askin' me for?"

"No reason." No, I didn't *actually* think Gourry was a conspiracy cracker in disguise, but it never hurts to ask. I shook my head, sharing in his general puzzlement over the way things stood.

"Honestly," I said, my spirits sagging, "I don't have a clue, either. Until that last attack, we weren't sure if the enemy was even after me personally." I gripped my chin. "Although," I said after thinking a bit, "if I'm the target, maybe it's got nothing to do with Phil and Christopher. Whoever's targeting me *could* just be using the whole palace situation as a cover."

Gourry frowned. "Maybe," he agreed after a second.

"Do you see why it'd be pointless for me to back out of all this? Whoever's after me is gonna stay after me regardless of where I go."

Gourry scratched his head, a sign that some of this was actually getting through that thick skull of his. "That's . . . true."

And I'll have to confront whoever it is eventually. I'd rather take my stand right here, where I have a job to finish."

I'd sure shut up Gourry. He stood there mutely, his eyes glazed over, his mouth a little open.

I paused. "Hey, Gourry?" I added.

"Yeah?"

"Thanks." I smiled at him. "I mean, for worrying about me. But I'll be okay."

Gourry sighed. "Be real careful, though," he told me. "There's a lot we don't know about Kanzeil. If he's really coming for you, we'd better be extra careful."

Gourry bringing up Kanzeil reminded me of something that had been bothering me ever since the bug brawl. "You know what's weird?" I found myself asking. "I know Kanzeil is one nasty and suspicious creep, but during that battle we just had, I'm sure he didn't cast a single spell."

Gourry's brow got all wrinkly. "Then how the hell . . ."

"I see what you mean," hummed Amelia, her arms folded. She paused to give Gourry a little while longer to figure it out, but he was busy trying to pick a piece of lint out of his hair.

"It means someone *else* summoned the demon." She gave him a forced smile. "Come on, Mr. Gourry—work with me here."

I cleared my throat. *Welcome to my world.* "Miss Amelia?" I asked. "Of all the others in the courtyard that afternoon, who can use magic?"

Amelia cocked her head, trying to remember. "Well," she said, "the escorts—I mean you and Mr. Gourry, if you count his magic sword—and Kanzeil, of course . . . then Uncle Christopher, Alfred, and myself." She paused. "In short, everybody except my father."

Now we were getting somewhere. "Can you tell me their power levels?"

"I'm not sure about the others," Amelia admitted. "For many of them, magic is just a hobby. I could tell you what spells they prefer but not really what level they're at.

"As for myself," she continued, "I mostly use Priestly Magic with some Black and Shamanic Magic thrown in. I learned from my older sister Gracia."

"Hmm," I said distantly. "That leaves one last person." I turned and locked eyes with Amelia. "I know there was once a guy here named Randy. If I remember correctly, he got on really well with Christopher, am I right?"

Amelia blinked, then nodded. "Well . . . yes. Except I wouldn't say he and Christopher got along *well,* they just managed to tolerate each other." She put her hands on her hips. "Miss Lina, I didn't know you knew Uncle Randionel."

"I knew him," I said vaguely, "a little." Okay, so it was an understatement.

I'd had a run-in with Randy before, and he was making me rethink my suspicions about Christopher summoning that beetle. *Randionel* had reason to be after me.

Awhile back, when I'd first met Phil, his traveling companion Randy—who just happened to be Third Successor to the Royal Throne—was trying to assassinate him. I got involved, yadda yadda yadda, and Randy's ass ended up kicked by none other than yours truly. I was starting to wonder if Christopher knew about all that.

Can't people just let bygones be bygones?

Argh. "Anyway," I said at last, letting out a long breath. "What ended up happening with Phil and Christopher's big meeting?"

"Oh." Amelia shrugged. "That got put on hold. Things were way too weird and stressed-out between Father and Uncle Christopher."

"So, after all that, we still don't know why I'm on a hit list?"

Amelia threw out her hands. "No no!" she exclaimed. "That's not the case at all!" She smiled again, but this time it was . . . impish.

"Kanzeil's vanished, Miss Lina."

***

145

The next time I saw Amelia was two days later. Gourry and I, figuring safety was in numbers, had decided to stick close to each other and to Phil—though tailing that guy could be a real snooze-fest for a gal who's used to the freedom of the road.

We were standing guard outside Phil's office and slowly losing sanity to boredom when she skipped up.

"Hey!" Amelia chirped with a smile. "How've you been?"

Amelia definitely took to the peace that had prevailed since the beetle debacle. Gourry and I were a little suspicious of the recent calm, but Amelia, for whatever reason, obviously wasn't.

She leaned in toward us and lowered her voice. "Come with me for a sec?"

Gourry and I shared a glance. "Sure."

She's being secretive now?

The three of us ducked into a nearby chamber. It was a guestroom, actually, not too different from the ones Gourry and I were staying in.

"What is it?" I asked in a low voice.

Amelia smiled. "Calm down," she reassured me. "It's nothing *that* serious." She produced a piece of paper from a pocket in her robe.

"It seems that yesterday," Amelia announced, "Lord Clawfell went into the city on an errand . . . and was abducted."

"He was *what*?"

Gourry, poor guy, was totally thrown off by Amelia's response. "Hold it," he said, actually holding out his hands. "Clawfell getting kidnapped *is* kinda serious, isn't it?"

I glared at Amelia incredulously. "I gotta agree with Gourry on this one."

"Well, that's why I'm brining you *this*."

It was a ransom letter addressed to Phil. As far as ransom notes go, it was strictly by-the-numbers, saying something to the effect that if Phil valued Clawfell's life, he was to appear at such-and-such appointed place and blah blah blah. Frankly, it made me yawn. Whoever was the ransom-note *auteur* sure didn't know how to tug on the strings of the desperate. Believe me, it can be fun.

"They probably don't like how well-guarded Father is right now," Amelia explained. "And if I know Father, the second he sees this he'll have to rush off to the rescue."

It didn't take me long to figure out where the conversation was headed. "Don't tell me," I said. "You want us to rescue Clawfell, right?"

"I knew I could count on you!" Amelia squealed happily. "I'm supposed to hand this letter over to Father right away, but I'll hold off until tomorrow evening. That should be enough time for you to rescue Clawfell and—"

"Hang on!" I broke in. "Amelia!" It was enough to put a stop to her incessant chittering. Looking her square in the eye and in as calm and rational a tone as I could muster, I said, "You do realize what you're asking, don't you? This is a helluva lot easier said than done."

Amelia frowned in an unsettlingly adorable fashion. "You don't want to do it?" she asked, still pouting.

I shuffled my feet. Gourry tried to avert his eyes, switching his gaze to the floor.

I sighed. "We'll do it," I answered, "but all I'm saying—"

"Yay!" Amelia smacked her palms together. "We're all set then!"

"But you do realize this is quite possibly a trap, don't you?"

Amelia waved her hand at me, a great big smile on her face. "Lina!" she exclaimed. "You big kidder! Of *course* it's a trap!"

Maybe I should take her faith in me as a compliment, I thought tiredly. After half a second of imagining where that would get me, I decided against it.

"Look," I muttered. "Think outside the box for a second, all right? The enemy might've sent this letter expecting that you'd show it to us. It's possible that they're planning to infiltrate the palace and attack *Phil* as soon as Gourry and I leave to rescue Clawfell."

She paused a minute. "Maybe," she agreed at last. Then she smiled again and said nothing more; I took that to mean she was done talking.

It was clear that Amelia didn't fear danger like normal, sane people did. She must've noticed that I was still anxious, because she placed a hand on my shoulder and said gently, "It's okay, Lina. I'm sure we'll get through this . . . probably."

Probably?!

"I realize," Amelia added, locking eyes with me, "that this mission puts you and Mr. Gourry at great risk. Lord Clawfell has been taken to a place that's very difficult for a large group of soldiers to surround—that's why I think the two of you are best qualified to handle things.

"Truly, I'd like to go with you. The desire to do so burns throughout my entire body like the Flames of Justice. But it's best that I stay here so that, if the need should arise, I can let fly with some necessary magic."

She let go of me and marched toward the door. Before leaving, she spun on her heels to face us.

"I know it's risky, but I really need for you to handle this yourselves. Please." She clasped her hands and, in a beseeching voice, added, "Pretty please."

With that, she turned and vanished out the door. I assumed she was off to tend to her flames . . . those raging Flames of Justice, that is.

Gourry and I stood there, staring blankly at each other. "Well," offered Gourry, "at least she said *pretty* please."

***

Thin fingers of fog curled through the city's narrow streets and alleys that night. Pale haloes of light from lampposts barely pierced through the fog's veil.

Block 15, Saillune City. The slum district.

The street was lined with dirty, frowning tenements. Lights winked from the taverns and the brothels, and I could hear the noise of rowdy and drunken revelers from within them. There was no one out in the street; obviously, the fear and tension that hung over other parts of Saillune City loomed over its slums as well.

Slipping out of the palace itself had been surprisingly easy—if we managed to rescue Clawfell, we could probably get back in through the main gate. The trouble was going to be in springing Clawfell from wherever he was. The thought of confronting Zuuma and another giant beetle didn't do much to strengthen my rescuing mood.

If Amelia's map was correct, the ransom rendezvous point was deep inside a spiderweb of alleyways. I realized now what Amelia had meant when she'd advised against a squad of soldiers; anyone familiar enough with the ins and outs of the maze of alleyways could easily outwit and escape a bulky pursuing force

We picked our way through as carefully as we could. The people who had kidnapped Clawfell had probably posted lookouts all over the place, so we had to be stealthy. I was in no mood for a surprise standoff that would alarm the district and blow the whistle on our whole mission.

Being smack dab in the middle of one of Saillune City's most crowded areas, the enemy definitely had the upper hand. Not only were they more familiar with the terrain but also less squeamish about wreaking serious havoc on innocent civilians. Plus, I was afraid their first tack would be to use Clawfell as a hostage.

I *did* have spells up my sleeve that I could use, but I couldn't be sure that someone as old as Clawfell could take that sort of thing without having a heart attack. Hence my finicky—okay, anal—insistence on being as exceedingly quiet and cautious as possible.

I stuck an arm out in front of Gourry. "Stop," I whispered.

Ahead of us was a large lamp-lit courtyard. My guess was that it had been made from the collapse or demolishment of several neighboring buildings. The ground was naturally unpaved, and in the center stood a single lamppost surrounded by garbage.

There were no two ways about it: Gourry and I had to cross through that place to get to our destination. I didn't like the idea of being exposed, especially since I could sense at least two hiding lookouts.

"Two people on the path ahead," Gourry muttered in a hushed voice.

"One's standing still," I said, "and the other's reporting to him. I think."

"Probably," Gourry agreed. He exhaled deeply. "Both of them seem decently tough."

"What do you mean, *decently?*" Gourry turned to me. "You remember those guys who attacked us at the guesthouse?" he whispered. "Not quite as tough, but close."

I groaned. "Kind of a problem, then." It wasn't so much a question of eliminating them—I was sure we could wipe the floor with those guys—but eliminating them *quietly*. I needed our mission to be as clean and silent as possible.

Gourry leaned in closer and asked, "Is there no other way through?"

"I might be wrong," I replied, "but I get the feeling they just changed shifts. If that's true, then we're wasting our time waiting; we have to break through."

"But how?"

I beckoned for him to bend down. Once he was closer, I cupped my hand around his ear and whispered the plan.

Half a minute later, Gourry and I marched straight into the courtyard. We kept our gait as casual as if we were just out for a breath of fresh, foggy air. On the other side, we saw the silhouettes of two figures standing watch. I was sure they'd noticed us, but in the dim lamplight and the fog we were probably pretty obscured.

"How you doin', fellas?" Gourry said in a slightly strained tone. "What's the, uh, word?"

Thue figures didn't respond. They looked at us and then at each other, probably bewildered that they were being spoken to. "The targets . . . left the Royal Palace," one of them said at last. "They should be here any minute."

Gourry and I nodded casually and kept walking toward the alley. As we drew closer, we could make out their forms more clearly.

"Why?" asked the same lookout. "Did something happen?"

"Don't scare us," the other lookout added. "We thought you were the enemy."

Gourry smiled as we stepped up to them. "We are," he quipped. In a whoosh of air and a crack of fist hitting face, Gourry reduced the first of them to an unconscious heap on the ground.

The second lookout could only blurt, "Wha?!" and bring a whistle to his lips before Gourry caught the back of his head with a hand-chop. The lookout slumped to his knees, wide-eyed and with a hand cupped around his throat, before he dropped face-first to the ground. I could hear the whistle that had gotten rammed down his throat making soft tweets as he breathed.

"Man," commented Gourry. "They sure *fell* for that one."

Knowing Gourry as well as I did, I was pretty sure he hadn't meant to make that terrible, terrible joke and I could therefore spare his life.

"The enemy probably hired a bunch of mercenaries from all over the place," I said as we picked our way around the lookouts. "It's no surprise they don't all know each other, particularly in the dark."

I felt a tinge of anxiety as we continued onward. "We'd better hurry," I added. "It won't be long before—" My words caught in my throat as a presence—a very *bad* presence— suddenly zapped into existence behind us.

Gourry and I spun around at the same time. There, under the wane light of the lamppost and wrapped in the green veil of fog, stood Kanzeil the Sorcerer. He calmly stared at us with his evil ice eyes.

"It's been awhile," he remarked. "Several days, I believe."

"Kanzeil," I answered, glaring back. " I thought you'd be long gone after ditching your employer and leaving the Royal Palace." I tried to stay calm, but how do you stay calm around a psychopath with talent? I still wasn't clear on exactly what kind of destruction the guy was capable of.

"Ditching my employer?" Kanzeil repeated from across the fog. "Not exactly. It seems that my *employer* didn't care for my methods, although I can't say I blame him." He watched his long fingers as he flexed them. "It's just as well. "I couldn't bring attention to myself, and my magic was too constrained. Many embarrassments ensued as a result."

I cleared my throat, trying to work up the nerve to actually say something. That guy was champing at the bit to wreak some havoc.

"Embarrassments?" I asked with as much confidence as I could muster. "What was he paying you for, Kanzeil?"

I heard the sound of Gourry unsheathing his Sword of Light. He was acting on instinct now, alert to a sensation I was beginning to feel myself: that Kanzeil was looking for the slightest opportunity to take us down for good. As far as villains go, Kanzeil was well on his way to giving me an ulcer.

"You should know the answer to that," he replied calmly, his lips curling in a smile reserved for the especially evil. "To *kill* you, Lina Inverse."

"But why? Why kill *me*?"

"That," Kanzeil said, smiling again as his form began to ripple, "is for me to know . . . and you to *die* for."

And with that, he vanished. Half a second later I felt his presence somewhere behind me.

I spun around and found myself staring at Kanzeil's open hand. A pale blue light flared up around it.

"Good-bye."

SAILLUNE: CAUGHT IN THE FAMILY FEUD

FOOM!

A brilliant ball of energy burst from Kanzeil's palm, only to scatter into showers of light before it slammed into my forehead. I heard the faint humming of Gourry's blade and realized that I'd been within a hair's breadth of getting barbequed.

Kanzeil wasn't kidding around. He hadn't even bothered with an elaborate trap or a speech about how he was invincible—the man just wanted blood. Gourry lashed at Kanzeil with the Sword of Light, but Kanzeil leapt backward and out of reach before vanishing again.

His presence zapped in directly above us. Instinctively, I jumped away from where I stood; glancing behind me I saw a shower of energy balls raining down on where I'd just been.

"Your instincts are sharp," Kanzeil boomed from above, his back against the night sky. "If you had looked up, you'd be a sizzling puddle of flesh right now."

I tried to snicker at Kanzeil, but it came out sounding more like a croak. "N-not in the mood to sizzle, thanks. And I like my flesh the way it is."

Honestly, I was floored. No one I'd ever encountered could chant a teleportation spell and then immediately launch an energy attack. Everything I'd learned about magic in books told me that wasn't possible.

For *humans*, anyway.

"Don't look so surprised," Kanzeil said as he floated gently to the ground.

Just as Kanzeil touched down, Gourry slashed Kanzeil from behind. Unfortunately, Kanzeil just vanished again, this time reappearing under the lamppost at the center of the courtyard.

"This is a trick even Seigram can handle," Kanzeil called. "It's really no great feat."

Gourry and I glanced at each other. Seigram, the Mazoku that Gourry and I had locked in a death-match with? We'd barely won that fight, and we definitely hadn't finished Seigram off. I had a feeling we'd cross paths with him again when he was thirsting for revenge.

Kanzeil spoke of Seigram so off-handedly, like he was nothing but a minion.

"Y-you're a Mazoku?!" Gourry cried.

Kanzeil chuckled. "Yes. And *you* are easily fooled. However, for a human to mistake the mere form of a human for humanity itself . . . that indeed is most human."

Just so you don't get the wrong idea, while Kanzeil was spewing scorn, I was chanting a spell under my breath. I knew that, at best, I might knock the wind out of him with one of my spells. But there's nothing like trying, right?

I was coming to realize that Kanzeil probably *had* been the one to summon the beetle. That damn thing had withstood a direct hit from my Atscha Dist spell, and any demon who could summon a creature that powerful had to be *ridiculously* powerful himself. The thought was frightening.

The only spell I thought might possibly beat Kanzeil was Dragon Slave, but it was far too lethal to summon in the middle of a densely populated area. Besides that, I had an assortment of other less destructive spells that could potentially damage a Mazoku, but their variety and power levels were pretty limited.

To defeat a Mazoku as powerful as Kanzeil would require me to strike him several times in quick succession. That was not a feat I had any illusions of accomplishing; Kanzeil was too fast and too crafty for that. With Gourry, though, and his Sword of Light, I figured I had a glimmer of a chance. That is *if* Gourry could get around Kanzeil's teleportation trick. But like I said, anything's worth a shot. And Gourry, obviously, was thinking the same thing.

"Let's go!" he cried as he sprang forward.

I followed close on his heels.

"That's a fairly impressive speed," Kanzeil commented as we rushed him. But, as expected, he vanished just as Gourry brought down his blade. The Sword of Light cleaved nothing but air.

Kanzeil's vanishing was my cue to get the hell away from where I was standing. I wasn't going to get fried into a crispy curl if I could help it. As I leapt away, I sensed Kanzeil to the right of the lamppost.

"Elmekia Lance!" I shouted and released my spell just as Kanzeil appeared.

"Please," Kanzeil sighed, sounding more bored than scornful. He muttered a single word and my magic lance burst apart in midair.

"Do you honestly think you'd have a chance with that?" he asked. "Let's not waste each other's time, shall we?" As he spoke, a brilliant light flashed forth from his body.

"OW!" I yelled, squinting my dark-adjusted eyes and throwing an arm over them. The back of my eyeballs burned as if every nerve ending had been singed, but I didn't have time to nurse the pain.

I leapt to my right. It must've been in the nick of time, because as I moved, I felt a hot mass—a fireball, maybe—

graze past my head. A couple of seconds later a nasty explosion went off not far behind me.

I'd managed to dodge another shot, but my luck wasn't going to hold out all night. My vision still hadn't recovered; everything was still a blur and my eyeballs hurt.

Suddenly, I sensed the presence of several new intruders in our midst.

More guys from the group that kidnapped Clawfell?

They'd probably heard all the commotion and decided to attack in large numbers.

"Lighting!" I managed to unleash my own blinding flash of light on the unsuspecting newcomers.

"Hey!" the men cried. I heard them tumble over each other, screaming about their eyes; in the alarm and confusion I ran right into the thick of them. I knew they wouldn't serve as much more than meat shields against a cruel bastard like Kanzeil, but I needed to buy time until my vision came back.

"Ugh," was Kanzeil's only audible comment. He grumbled a bit more, but then vanished.

Where would he appear next? I desperately scanned the area for his presence, but came up with nothing. What I *did* sense were several other intruders—probably more of Clawfell's kidnappers—approaching from the other side of the alley. My vision was slowly coming back; I still couldn't see much, but at least my eyeballs hadn't melted away.

"Lina!" It was Gourry's voice. I felt his hand grab mine and pull me away from the hullabaloo.

He clutched both my shoulders and stared at me. "You all right?!" Apparently his vision had come around a lot sooner than mine.

"Somehow," I muttered, blinking and squinting. "Kanzeil . . . ?"

"I dunno—he didn't come back after the last time he vanished. Can you walk?"

I nodded. "But I'm still pretty blind," I added. "I can't swing a sword, but I think I'll manage."

"More enemies are heading this way. There's no way we can break through their ranks, not in this alleyway. Can you make us fly?"

"I'll try." I began to chant. Until our recent episode with Kanzeil, I'd been careful not to use magic for fear that our enemies would sense us. But now, after our not-so-quiet run-in with Kanzeil and blinding a slew of guys with Lighting, any idiot who *couldn't* sense us was probably dead.

I clung to Gourry. "Ray Wing!" I shouted, and toward the rooftops we soared.

"Congratulations on making it this far," boomed a man positioned at the entrance of the old stone-and-brick apartment building Gourry and I were making for. He puffed his chest out arrogantly. "You're pluckier than I thought."

Ordinarily, I'd have had no qualms knocking the bozo flat on his face. But the dark apartment building behind him was huge, and not knowing which room Clawfell had been stashed in meant a blind search would take all night. Besides, flipping over every chair and table would only alert the kidnappers and let them slip away with Clawfell.

I sighed and lowered us to the ground.

Stupid diplomacy. Now I have to threaten and/or kick the snot out of one of these guys so he'll bring me to Clawfell.

The authoritative monkey with the puffed-out chest would do just fine. "Hey there, champ," I addressed him. "Listen, we don't have time to shoot the breeze, so let's get right to it, shall we? Just hand over the old guy and we'll consider not killing you. How's that?"

The man considered my words calmly, a little too calmly for my taste. "Now, now," he chuckled. "That's no way to talk to someone who's just taken your friend hostage."

"It is . . . if you know you can shatter every bone in his body without half trying, so I suggest you cut the attitude.

And if we find that you've killed Clawfell already, that'll only make the decision to tear you to confetti that much easier."

"You've got me quakin' in my boots," the man replied in a mocking tone. "Don't worry, girlie, our hostage is too valuable to kill. He's sittin' pretty." The man stepped toward us, and with a sweep of his hand said, "But I wouldn't try anything if I were you. See, I've got lookouts posted all over this place. If they see you start somethin', they've been instructed to chop little pieces off that geezer pal of yours."

"Wha?!" Gourry and I both cried at once.

"So unless you want your buddy missin' fingers and toes, you'd best behave yourselves." The man chuckled and shook his head. "We're all outsiders, darlin', and not one of us is gonna think twice about slicin' and dicin' the old man if it comes down to it."

"Damn," I muttered under my breath. The monkey knew how to use a hostage, which wasn't something I'd expected.

"So, girlie?" the man snarled, baring a lovely set of broken yellowed teeth.

Ugh! Learn to floss, stinky.

"Fine." I turned to Gourry. "We'd better lose the weapons, Gourry." Gourry sighed, dismayed. "Guess so," he murmured.

We both tossed our weapons aside. Half a second later, a bunch of men swarmed out of the building and tied our hands behind our backs.

"For a pair of badasses, we got captured pretty fast, don't ya think?" Gourry asked.

"Like we had a choice," I muttered back. "We'll get out of this. We always do."

"You *are* tied up, right?"

"Shut yer yappin'," one of the men drawled. "Less talky more walky." He was acting like this was the most boring job he'd ever had.

We were led deep into the bowels of the foul-smelling building and over to a grimy apartment building. The flickering torchlight brightened the interior of the empty room; molding mud-stained walls and the stink of raw garbage were among the place's most charming features.

I had to hold my breath against the stink.

"Look," I said to one of the rogues, "all I wanna know is if Clawfell's really safe. I promise to shut up if you tell me."

The rogue smirked. "You'll be meetin' him soon enough."

"I've heard that one before," I snapped.

The rogue snickered. "Don't worry," he assured in his sandpaper voice. "We won't kill him until we get what we want."

"Until he's not *useful* to you anymore, you mean."

"Think what you want, girlie."

I had just about had it with all that *girlie* garbage. Someone was gonna have to pay the piper, courtesy of yours truly.

Gourry and I were led to the back of the room and out a door that looked like some sort of back exit. Beyond the door was a crumbling, winding stairway that led only one way—down.

"Oho; the basement, I see."

"Shut up," grunted the rogue.

We proceeded single file down the stone steps; the air becoming steadily more damp. A solitary door awaited us at the foot of the stairway.

"We're here," the rogue snapped, then pushed open the door.

I froze.

Of all the people on the planet that could've been behind that door, he was probably in the bottom five with Phil and Shabranigdu.

"I've been waiting for you," Zuuma murmured. I stared at him, my eyes wide, my flesh crawling.

"What the—what do *you* want?" the rogue blurted. He clearly didn't expect Zuuma, either. Maybe there was something (or someone) else hidden in that basement, but with Zuuma just behind the doorway, I couldn't see a damn thing.

"I'm here to kill the girl," Zuuma replied in his unflappable tone. "Give her to me."

"Like hell!" barked the roque. "You're an assassin hired by that Kanzeil, ain't ya? I've got news for ya—Kanzeil's not a part of our team anymore, so that makes you unwelcome around here. And as for these two," he gestured to Gourry and me, "they're important prisoners of ours. So, you'd best get on outta here."

It wasn't as if the rogue had suddenly rushed to my defense. He just had his feathers ruffled by Zuuma, and now he wanted to mouth back. Too bad all he was really doing was hastening his own death.

"I see," Zuuma uttered as he stepped out of the room, narrowing the gap between him and the masochistic smart-ass. "Since I have no allegiance to you whatsoever, it shall be an easy matter to do away with you." Then, with a calm sort of malevolence, he floated slightly upward.

SWISH!

Something lashed out from Zuuma. It happened too fast for me to catch the details, but I *really* didn't need any as the rogue's body slumped to the floor . . . and his head rolled elsewhere.

Zuuma, still hovering just above the ground, pivoted in my direction.

Crap!

He flew in a graceful arc and deceptively fast. The other kidnappers had been thrown into total terror and confusion and frantically tried to rally for a fight. I didn't have much time to think myself, so I stumbled backward, chanting a spell.

"Whaaa!" cried one of the men as he lunged toward Zuuma. Well, not so much *lunged* as *got thrown*. Gourry had manged to deliver a mule-kick straight into his back, sending the man headlong at Zuuma.

Caught off-guard by the body flung at him, Zuuma tried to dodge it. But the corridor was too narrow, and a second later the man's airborne body crashed into Zuuma's and sent the two of them tumbling back into the room.

"Why you!" yelled another rogue.

A mini mob of kidnappers stampeded past me and into the room, shouting curses and war cries amid the trampling of their boots. It gave me the chance to finish chanting my spell.

"Braham Fang!"

The Wind Arrows I shot sliced easily through the ropes binding Gourry. He didn't waste any time rushing to the headless corpse, grabbing our confiscated swords, and running back to free me.

***

The battle was on its last legs by the time Gourry and I rushed past it. I wanted to know what the kidnappers had been storing in that place—and, sure enough, in the center of the cellar sat Clawfell, bound to a chair.

Finally! Time to get this show on the road!

Clawfell's glum face switched to delight. "Oh!" he piped up. "You two!" He certainly *looked* fine, and it seemed safe enough to move toward him, but Gourry and I didn't get the chance. A lighting spell illuminated the freshly killed bodies, strewn in tangled heaps all over the floor. And, in the midst, stood a less-than-apologetic Zuuma.

Gourry leaned in toward me. "Do you think we can beat that guy?" he whispered.

"Dunno," I replied. I'm usually pretty sure about our chances going into a fight—and I usually know we're going to win—but with Zuuma, the odds weren't exactly in our favor.

Zuuma turned to us with the same malicious deliberation he'd had with his last beheading. "Step aside," he told Gourry calmly.

Gourry positioned himself between me and Zuuma, his blade ready for combat. "You didn't say 'pretty please,' " he answered flatly.

Gourry slowly began to advance. Zuuma, probably sensing Gourry's capabilities, moved carefully.

The thing that worried me the most was Zuuma's darkness spell—the one he'd used back in my bedroom. If he cast it here, Gourry wouldn't stand a chance.

I chose the best preventative measure I could think of: I sprinted across the room toward Clawfell.

Zuuma, startled at my sudden movement, diverted his attention to me for a spilt second. It was all the opportunity Gourry needed; charging with lightning speed, he slashed at the assassin with a loud cry. Zuuma barely leapt backward, but he still managed to dodge the reach of Gourry's sword.

Damn!

But Gourry wasn't deterred, and he wasn't going to give Zuuma a chance to counterattack. He immediately charged and swung at Zuuma again, effectively backing the assassin up against the wall.

In a fight, you couldn't find a smarter swordsman than Gourry; he had slashed with everything he had the second Zuuma was cornered. Unfortunately, Zuuma just dropped to the ground and rolled full force at Gourry.

Against your average opponent, a succession of kicks and sword swipes will stop him from rolling anywhere ever again. But against Zuuma, a stunt like that'll only lead to you losing your foot.

Gourry quickly leapt backward to get some distance between him and Zuuma. With Gourry in retreat, Zuuma uncoiled himself, jumped to his feet, and began sprinting full speed—at *me*!

"Dammit!" I heard Gourry yell. I brandished my sword while hurriedly casting a spell. As Zuuma ran across the floor, he jumped up and, in a single motion, pushed his palms off the ceiling and propelled a powerful kick in my direction.

I didn't feel like losing my head, so I didn't dare attempt a counter-offense. Instead, to save my neck—quite literally—I flung myself away from Zuuma's attack.

"Lighting!"

It took me a second to realize that neither Zuuma nor I had cast the spell. But Clawfell had!

The old guy couldn't have picked a better time or aimed any truer. A brilliant orb of light shot across the room and slammed directly into Zumma, burning his eyes.

"Arrgh!" Zuuma grunted as he buried his face in his hands.

I know how bad that hurts, buddy!

Zuuma staggered halfway across the room, reeling from the attack. He must've figured he was momentarily outmatched, because the next thing he did was back away toward the door. With a final hiss in our direction, he spun around on his heels and sprinted up the steps.

Gourry ran to the door with his sword in hand, but paused in the doorway. Like me, he figured we were in no position to pursue an enemy who could obviously have us for breakfast. "Looks like we chased him off," Gourry said somewhat incredulously, peering up the stairway. "Who'da thought, huh?"

I got to untying the ropes that bound Clawfell to his chair. "I owe you my life, Mr. Clawfell," I murmured as I worked. Honestly, if he hadn't cast the lighting spell when he had, who knows if I'd still be around to tell the tale.

"Now, now," said Clawfell pleasantly. "I'm the one who ought to be thanking you. That lighting spell is the only spell I know, and up 'til now all it's ever been good for is reading in the middle of the night."

With a stiff grunt, Clawfell stood up from the chair. He tossed the loose rope away and rubbed his sore wrists. You could see the ruts and burns that the binding had left in them.

Wearily, Clawfell scanned the bodies strewn about the floor. "There must be survivors among the fallen here."

Clawfell was right. After we checked the bodies, we found that a handful of them were merely unconscious. We couldn't say the same for the others, though. Their butchered body parts were strewn about, mixed up like some morbid jigsaw puzzle. All in all, there were four survivors, so we immediately tied them up. One of them came to as Gourry was securing him. The rogue looked disoriented, and as he groaned and rolled his eyes, I could see him trying to figure out where he was and what had happened.

"Hiya," I said, smacking him on the shoulder. "How you feelin', old boy?" I tried to sound as ruthless as I could, which isn't always easy when you're as cute as I am.

"Y-you?" he breathed, his eyes bugging out of his head. "I get it now. That goddamn Kanzeil! He hired us and then double-crossed us!"

He trained his crazed eyes at me and then at Gourry. He looked so scared I almost felt sorry for him . . . but if he was under the impression that Kanzeil was behind what happened, Gourry and I weren't about to correct him. The situation was beginning to turn in our favor, you could say.

"Oh, shut up!" I snapped. "You knew the risks when you took the job. Gotta watch your back in this business, got me?!"

The prisoner stared at the dead on the floor—the pieces of them, I mean—and moaned, his lips trembling. "Are they . . . dead?"

No, they're just unwinding after a long day!

"Do they look alive to you?!" I barked. "And if you're not careful, pal, you're gonna be joining them just like that!" I snapped my fingers commandingly. I can't really snap that well, but I don't think he noticed.

"No, please!" the rogue implored. "Spare me!"

"Then get talking. Who hired you?!"

"I-I don't know!" he blurted. "Really! I'm not lying!"

A pretty standard attempt at denial by a desperate prisoner, and I wasn't buying it.

"I see," I said, a delicious iciness in my voice.

Man, I'm beginning to enjoy this!

"If you don't know," I continued, pacing slowly with my hands clasped behind my back, "then we have no choice."

I leaned forward, changing my tone to devilish. "There are three others alive here. I'll just ask them." And then, turning to Gourry, I said, "Why don't you chop this one up? He's no help to us."

The prisoner's face turned green.

Following my bluff, Gourry walked up behind him, ran a finger around the prisoner's neck, then unsheathed his sword.

"Wait!" the man howled. "Wait! I'll tell you anything! Whaddaya wanna know?!"

"But I thought you didn't know anything?" I hummed.

"I'll tell you everything I know! Please, just let me live!"

I folded my arms and paced around to make it appear as if I was considering the man's appeal. Judge me if you will, but it was the most fun I'd had in a long time and I think I freakin' earned it.

"Hmm," I said at last. "All right, talk. If I like what I hear, I'll spare you."

"You wanna know who's pullin' the strings, right?!" the prisoner offered frantically. "You guys probably know him your-self. He's one of those snot-nosed Royals; he always came to us in disguise and never said who he was. But I heard him talkin' to Kanzeil once and Kanzeil said his name."

I yawned. "We know it's Christopher, so spare us the suspense, pal."

"It's not Christopher," the rogue contested. He suddenly smiled, and might've even looked sly if he hadn't still been shaking. "It's *Alfred*."

"What?!" Gourry, Clawfell, and I shouted in unison.

I blinked a few times and shook my head like I'd just fallen on it.

Alfred? Mr. Priss himself?

"It's true," our prisoner quickly assured us. "In fact, he'd badmouthed his dad every chance he got."

"But Alfred was with us when we were attacked at the guesthouse," I thought aloud. "Why would he have been there?!"

The prisoner smirked. "Oh, yeah . . . *that*."

Obviously, he had some dirt to spill on that too.

"I know there was a team for that job picked out of our ranks. It was a last-minute thing, but with help from our palace contact, the team still snuck into the complex easily." The man paused for breath. "Anyway," he went on, "they were instructed to attack once they got the signal—some sort of pounding. The only other instruction was to leave a certain someone unharmed."

Some sort of pounding?

Of course! I remembered how Alfred—in a show of desperation—had slammed his fists on the table back in the guesthouse moments before the sabotage. All that hell breaking loose, and Alfred still got to look like an innocent victim.

The gears in my brain were beginning to turn. "What else?" I pressed the prisoner. While his tongue was loose, I wanted him to spill as much as he could.

"Our plans were going peachy at first. But then Kanzeil started pullin' his show-off crap, like launching his own attacks and messin' up our strategy. Conspiracy's an art, y'know? So we dropped him."

"How'd Kanzeil and Alfred get to know each other, anyway?" I asked.

The prisoner shook his head. "How should I know? All I know is Alfred set this whole thing up."

I had to admit the man's story held up. Kanzeil had probably caught wind of my acquaintanceship with Phil; figuring I would help Phil if there were assassination attempts on him, Kanzeil smooth-talked Alfred into going after the throne.

So Kanzeil engineered an entire royal conspiracy just to get to me?

It seemed like a roundabout way to track me down . . . but, in Kanzeil's defense, the task of finding someone with my kind of wanderlust and mad skills can be near impossible.

"What else?" I asked the prisoner brusquely. "Speak up!"

The man shook his head. Clearly, we'd wrung every drop from him.

So, we had our witness, which left us with hauling in the prisoners. The rogue had to repeat to Phil what he'd confessed to Gourry, Clawfell, and myself. The rest would be for Phil to decide. As for Gourry and me, our work would be done, and we could finally beat it out of Saillune City.

Only two nagging problems remained. For one: there was no shaking off Kanzeil and Zuuma—a showdown was coming, probably sooner rather than later. And as for the other problem . . .

Gourry must've sensed I was lost in thought. "What is it, Lina?" he asked. "You don't look too happy. We got what we wanted, didn't we?"

"Mmm," I groaned. "Sorta."

"You're worried about Kanzeil, aren't you?"

I inhaled deeply and nodded. No matter how upbeat things had turned out for us that night with Clawfell and the breakthrough regarding Alfred, it couldn't supplant my fear of an inevitable fight with a Mazoku and his super-powerful assassin.

With the four survivors in tow, Gourry, Clawfell, and I made our way out of the building and back toward the Royal Palace. The streets outside were mistier and way too quiet. Which brought us to our second problem: Alfred's thugs who might come at us with an attack more lethal than any of the previous attempts.

Why can't a girl just go home and catch some shut-eye after a job well done? No rest for the weary, I tell ya.

Then, just ahead of us and right in our path, I noticed dark human shapes; about thirty or forty of them loomed in the fog. One of them stepped forward from the rest. I must admit I was a little surprised when I saw who it was.

"How nice of you to wait for us, Alfred," I said flatly. He ran his fingers through his thick, styled locks and huffed at me with a toss of his head.

"I've indeed been eagerly awaiting you, my lady," he drawled.

I arched an eyebrow at him. "Though I must admit, I didn't expect you to show up in person. Awfully gracious of you to do us this honor."

"My dear Lina," he replied, "it was the least I could do to show my admiration for the little girl who found me out."

"It musta come as quite a shock," I offered.

Alfred breathed through his flared nostrils, clearly aggravated. I was loving it.

"It's been frustrating to no end," Alfred said through gritted teeth, "to have one's plans foiled at every turn."

"It's awfully late, Alfred. Shouldn't you be putting your hair to bed?"

"Think you're real cute, don't you, darling?"

"I could go on all night if you like."

"I think not." Alfred's scowl melted away, and was instead replaced with an icy smile. "I'm not in the mood for words. I'd rather watch you die."

I drew my sword. "Bring it on," I replied evenly.

From behind us, hidden in fog, an all-too-familiar voice intoned, "Let me handle the girl."

Can't this guy ever give it a rest?!

"Zuuma?" Alfred snorted. "Well . . . so long as she ends up dead, I don't care *who* does it. But this doesn't mean I like you!" Alfred pointed as menacingly as a priss can manage. "And it doesn't mean I forgive you for butting into my plans!"

Alfred's little display of super-villainy was getting sadder by the moment. I turned around to the much bigger threat. Zuuma stood not far behind us, shrouded in fog and clad in black. Our way had become barricaded on both sides by very unfriendly forces.

Which meant violence, and lots of it.

"Let's cut the crap and get down to business," Gourry said boldly. He drew his Sword of Light and aimed its tip at Zuuma. "If you wanna fight Lina, you're gonna have to get through me first."

Zuuma fell silent for a moment, turning his gaze from Gourry to me, then back to Gourry. "Then through you I shall go," he answered at last.

Zuuma was an incredibly skilled assassin, but there was no way he could take me out with Gourry all over him. He probably figured he had to focus his energies on Gourry while Alfred kept me busy. He and Gourry stared at each other, on guard and deliberately unmoving.

Alfred impatiently smacked his palms together. "Anytime, gentlemen! I want to get to bed soon!"

Speaking of getting to bed.

"Sleeping!" I had to prevent the prisoners from butting into my business.

As they passed out, Gourry leapt for Zuuma, and I charged the mob. And yes, it *was* a rather impressive bit of unspoken coordination—thank you for noticing.

"Attack!" commanded Alfred.

The ranks of soldiers, silhouetted in the fog, suddenly began to charge like one giant wave. But I had already begun chanting, so I plunged right into them with my sword.

"Mega Brand!"

A ripple erupted in the stone paving beneath the thugs' feet. The ground itself heaved, flipping and hurling hoodlums skyward. That took care of quite a few of them and gave me a chance to pull back and prepare my next spell.

Should I just take Alfred hostage? I wondered as I chanted. But that entailed the risk of Alfred's men taking *Clawfell* hostage, and I wasn't in the mood for a ring of hostage-taking. Oh, well—direct is usually best.

"Van Ga Ruim!" Alfred suddenly shouted, his arms raised high above him,

An insectlike buzz radiated from a black mist forming around Alfred's feet. Inhuman shapes began to rise from the darkness, quivering ominously.

Shadow beasts! *Lovely.*

Shadow beasts are low-ranking demons summoned from the astral plane. They're like zombies or leaches, attaching themselves to targets to drain out life force. They're pretty unstable creatures that'll fizzle out in half a day without anything to suck on, but that didn't make my situation any better.

Shadow beasts may be low-ranking, but physical attacks and elemental magic still do zilch against them. *And* it was too late for me to change my spell.

"Fireball!" I yelled.

I knew full well that inflicting fireballs on shadow beasts was a big waste of time, so I shifted the direction of my attack toward the thugs. "Break!" I commanded, focusing my attentions on the orb.

The fireball fragmented into ten tinier balls, each of which caused a petite but potent explosion. It had the desired effect, sending the rogues scattering in all sorts of directions.

The good news: half the guys were knocked out of commission or dead. The bad news: the other half was getting more desperate. What I really needed was time—if the city guardsmen caught wind of the melee, they'd surely come running and give me the advantage I was seeking.

One of the goons slashed at me, but I managed to parry his blade with mine and push him away. That gave me a fraction of a second to work my magic.

"Dust Chip!"

Pockets of air surrounding the lamppost lights began to glitter. I ducked out of the way.

A huge array of ice darts—all shiny, pointy, and about the size of a big toe—shot out at my attackers. They aren't really lethal, of course, but they still hurt like hell.

"Diem Wing!" It was Alfred this time. He'd chanted a shockwave spell: a violent gust of wind meant to knock opponents off balance. It's a difficult spell to evade because of its wide area, so all I could do to minimize its impact was leap as far away from its center (Alfred) as I could.

Whoosh!

A spasm of wind raged past me as the shockwave surged through. I couldn't catch my breath for the few seconds that it hit; that was enough for the shadow beasts to start closing in.

Dammit! I thought as I regripped my sword. If I could just get a minute to chant a *good* spell, I could raze those shadow beasts without a problem. But Alfred's strategy, it seemed, was to deploy his spells in short bursts just to keep me off my groove.

"Ugh!"

My blood went cold. Clawfell! I spun around to see his sword spin through the air before clattering on the ground.

Clawfell was attempting to stumble away from an advancing thug. The rogue cackled like an evil ten-year-old, raising his sword above his head as I quickly chanted a support spell.

"Say your prayers, gramps!" he cried.

"Braham Blazer!" A blue flare of light blazed through the night and mowed down the thug just in time. It was very dramatic and awfully slick, but there was just one problem: *I* didn't cast the spell.

Even Alfred was shocked. "What?" he exclaimed, frantically looking around. "Who threw that?!"

A silhouette stood poised on the second-floor verandah of a dilapidated house. The figure stepped into the light and folded her arms.

Yeah, I was as surprised as you are.

"Hmph!" Amelia uttered, her priestess robes swishing. "You, of all people, need to ask?"

4 : LET'S SETTLE IT HERE AND NOW

"Amelia!" Alfred cried. His eyes nearly popped out of his well-groomed head. "What are *you* doing here?!"

Amelia placed her hands firmly on the verandah's railing. "You could trick the entire world," she declared, "but nothing fools these Eyes of Justice!" Singing a bit of her own fanfare, she threw off her priestess' robes to reveal white, flowing fighter's garb.

She then turned and disappeared into a doorway. I heard her running in the halls inside the house, only to suddenly appear on the verandah again with her arms outstretched. She grasped the rail and lifted herself high up into an arcing somersault.

"Ooo!" Amelia cried out jubilantly as the rest of us looked on.

I gotta admit, the girl had her acrobatics down. Amelia soared through the air, flipping gracefully, but it didn't seem . . . no, she definitely wasn't timing her descent too well—

SPLAT!

Amelia didn't quite stick the landing. And by "didn't stick" I mean "plowed face-first into the dirt yard that fronted the old house."

Ouch!

After an uncomfortably long pause, Amelia finally got to her feet and dusted herself off. She sauntered on over to us, cool as a cucumber, like the most painful pratfall I'd ever seen hadn't just happened.

Well . . . she's got spunk, at least. Then again, she is Phil's daughter, and Phil is surprisingly tough for a mangy old coot.

Amelia defiantly pointed a finger at Alfred. "You've gone far enough, Al!" she declared. "Give yourself up right now or else!"

"Dammit!" Alfred cursed through clenched teeth. "How'd you find out?!"

Amelia crossed her arms. "I followed you out here! I couldn't sleep tonight and decided to go for a walk in the

courtyard, but then I noticed you sneaking out of the complex and smelled something fishy. I tracked you until you met up with a group of slimeballs and picked a fight with Miss Lina and the others. That's when it came to me—you're actually evil!"

That conclusion would've come to a comatose *monkey* at that point, but whatever. I suddenly wondered how long Amelia had been standing there. Had she been twiddling her fingers up on that verandah, watching us get creamed and waiting 'til Clawfell got in a pinch before intervening? Can someone say *bonehead?!*

Unlike me, Alfred seemed to take her speech pretty seriously. He ran a hand through his locks and snorted.

"Fine," he replied. "You mean I can go ahead and kill you as well? Good!" Rage suddenly flared up in his eyes.

"Don't get excited, Alfie, you might hurt something," I snapped. "Besides, you don't want people to think you are a second-rate villain who likes to pick on little girls."

"Villain?!" Alfred rebutted angrily. He cackled ominously, way louder than he needed to. "Don't be ridiculous! A commoner like you couldn't possibly understand the justice I'm doing! If I become king, this nation will become prosperous beyond its wildest dreams and gain its rightful place as head of the world! I'm no villain—I'm a leader, a dreamer!"

I rolled my eyes. Had I said second-rate? He didn't even deserve the compliment.

"Is that right?" Amelia challenged. She strode forward. "If justice is indeed what you possess, then you can prove it by defeating me!"

With Amelia distracting Alfred's attention, I could focus on protecting Clawfell and making mincemeat of Alfred's underlings. We suddenly had a shot at making it through the night alive. Clawfell, probably realizing how much of a liability he was alone, quickly ran to my side.

While all this was going on, Gourry and Zuuma were locked in on each other like a couple of wildcats. I didn't envy Gourry's position, but my hunch was that Gourry, with his Sword of Light, was better equipped than I was for a rumble like that.

The two fought in a cycle of attack-and-retreat: Gourry charged with his sword and drove Zuuma back, then Zuuma counterattacked with a spell and sent Gourry ducking for cover.

"Sheesh," I heard Gourry grunt, "this isn't working." Zuuma didn't reply, so Gourry slashed out again and forced Zuuma to lurch backward. The assassin raised his hands for another spell.

"Dark Mist!" Inky darkness swirled from Zuuma, crawling out to envelop the surrounding area.

"Whoa!" Gourry shouted as he quickly withdrew. From out of the darkness, a shadow took shape. It hovered silently for a second, thick and opaque, before leaping through the black mists and heading straight for Gourry.

"Haa!" Gourry grunted as he buried his sword deep into the shadow. Unfortunately, the shadow wasn't Zuuma, but a rogue corpse! Zuuma had thrown one of the dead men from the ground like a literal meat shield. With Gourry momentarily distracted, Zuuma shot from the cloud and made right for him.

If his opponent had been anyone lesser than Zuuma and his sword anything less priceless than the Sword of Light, Gourry would've had no qualms throwing his weapon aside and grappling free-handed. But it *was* Zuuma and he *did* hold the magic hilt, so Gourry hesitated for a split second . . . and, making my suspense even worse, I suddenly lost track of their movements in all the surrounding fury and confusion.

I did catch a glimpse of Zuuma launching himself in the air; with his arms circling in wide arcs, he whipped his legs at Gourry. Clang!

The near-deafening sound of cloven metal rang through the air. Blocking Zuuma's kick with his blade had, apparently, cost Gourry a blade. The force of the attack sent Gourry hurtling down the street with his broken sword in hand.

That's when I heard Alfred cry, "Flare Arrow!"

I pushed off the rogue I was fighting and whipped back to Amelia. A barrage of ten flaming arrows shot toward her in the night, but they each bounced away just inches in front of her. Turned out Amelia had already summoned Wind Barrier.

I physically felt my heart start up again. I was impressed by Amelia's quick thinking and Gourry's fortitude against Zuuma, but watching both fights was gonna give me a stroke.

"What?!" Alfred barked, his foppish face twisted in anger. He quickly began chanting a follow-up spell. Since Amelia's Wind Barrier was obviously powerful enough to deflect smaller attacks, there were no two ways about it—Alfred had to kick the battle up a *big* notch.

Amelia was, at the same time, beset by an array of those pesky shadow beasts. But I have to hand it to her; she didn't lose control. Instead, without flinching or panicking, she quietly chanted a new spell and finished reciting it before Alfred could make his next move.

"Diskang!" Alfred shouted.

The spell caused Alfred's shadow, which was caused by the lighting spells emanating from the lampposts, to grow to immense proportions. The monstrous shadow took the shape of a dragon's head. I knew what that meant—that dragon was a low-ranking astral plane demon. Lighting spell would be useless against it.

Not good!

The shadow dragon, its huge maw opened wide, advanced toward Amelia.

Needless to say, I was still protecting Clawfell and kicking thug ass while all this went on. The lackeys were a cinch to fend off one-by-one, but their sheer number kept me too preoccupied to direct any attack spells to aid the others.

"Man!" I groaned. "No saves, no glory, no fun!"

I launched a spell at several incoming hoodlums and wondered if Gourry was all right. It looked like his breastplate had taken the brunt of Zuuma's kick, so that was good news. The bad news was that skidding across the ground from the force of the kick had still left Gourry with a lot of nasty bruises.

Gourry cursed, leaping back to his feet. Zuuma made an immediate beeline for him; gripping his halved sword in his right hand, Gourry tucked his left hand along his flank and retreated farther.

"Fireball!" Zuuma called.

A ball of pale-blue light sprung forth from Zuuma's chest. At that instant, two things happened almost simultaneously: Gourry pitched something lefty, and Zuuma quickly bent his body backward.

ROAR!

An explosion ripped through the air and lit up the night sky. Gourry had thrown a rock at Zuuma's emerging fireball, causing an impact right in front of Zuuma's face.

As the flames evaporated in the night air, Zuuma emerged from the columns of smoke. But Gourry, by then, was ready for him; he surged forward, his broken sword glinting as he slashed.

"Flow Break!" Amelia's voice boomed impressively, loud and clear over the battle racket. The ground beneath her began to glow brightly; it was the same kind of luminescence lighting spells emanate, but Amelia had cast something far more effective.

An instant later, the points of a large hexagram pulsated out from the glowing aura and spread widely in all directions. On contact with the light, the dragon shadow and shadow beasts blinked out of existence, leaving a dumbfounded Alfred standing alone with his jaw slack. Then, as quickly as the hexagram appeared, it vanished.

Want me to explain that one, do ya? Amelia's spell had worked a lot like the one I'd used to break free from Kanzeil's space distortion: the hexagram's warding field had temporarily opened a portal to the astral plane and forced back a natural balance. That means that any and all demons—whose existence in our world is unnatural and unstable—had been pushed back to their own realm where they belong.

"Th-this can't be!" Alfred sniveled as he took a step back. He darted his eyes this way and that, clearly unable to believe what he was seeing—or, really, *wasn't* seeing. By the time he focused his attention back on Amelia, she was already in his face.

"Wha?!

Amelia cracked his jaw hard with her elbow. Alfred's head snapped back, and with a weak groan he went down like a sack of bricks.

Way to go, Amelia!

I was impressed—the girl had settled her score with that scheming little worm and didn't even break a sweat.

"This one's for you," I announced to Amelia as I bludgeoned the last of Alfred's men with an abandoned shield. The soldier folded like an accordion and went down in a heap.

That just left Gourry's fight with Zuuma. I turned to see Gourry lunging at the assassin with his broken sword and a loud cry.

"Haa!"

Even if his sword had been at full length, Gourry's attempt still would've been a stretch—Zuuma was too far and definitely too crafty to fall for an attack like that. But as I looked closer, I realized that Gourry was a step ahead of us all. As he charged, he slashed with his sword and simultaneously released the blade's clasp, launching the jagged piece of steel at Zuuma.

Zuuma's arm moved in a blur, streaking in front of him and deflecting the airborne blade with a sharp ding. The steel glinted as it spun away to clatter elsewhere in the darkness.

But before I had the chance to say, "Whoa," Gourry made his move. Zuuma's near-superhuman deflection had still given Gourry the split-second window of opportunity he needed.

"Light come forth!"

A blazing shaft of light burst from the sword hilt. Startled by the sight of the Sword of Light in action, Zuuma twisted his body and tried to hurl himself out of the way. But he wasn't fast enough. Not this time.

"Aagh!"

The light blade caught Zuuma's shoulder, cleaving through flesh and bone like a knife through butter. Zuuma staggered backward, grunting and panting, then gripped the scorched nub of bone on his right shoulder. Gourry had lopped the arm clean off at the joint.

Not only had Zuuma lost a limb, he'd obviously lost the fight. His expression turned from wide-eyed shock to bitter resignation. He staggered backward a bit before spinning around and leaping away, but I wasn't about to let him bolt so easily. That prick hadn't yet felt the fury of Lina Inverse—ready or not, he was gonna get a load of it now!

"Flare Lance!" I shouted.

Guessing his escape route, I unleashed my spell the instant Zuuma began to sprint down the street. There was no way he could dodge that spell with one arm . . . but that's the trouble with badass assassins. They do all sorts of things they shouldn't be able to.

Zumma whirled around and jerked up his remaining arm, parrying the lance an instant before impact. The lance exploded in a shower of red sparks, flash-burning his arm and pretty much vaporizing it into ash.

It was a nasty sacrifice, but better to lose your other arm than your life, I guess. Zuuma spun back around, now *completely armless*, and vanished off down the road.

I let out the breath I'd unconsciously been holding.

Whatever . . . I think that bastard earned his escape.

Amelia wiped the dust off her hands. "Well!" she chirped. "I'd say justice has been done here!"

I nodded, a little reluctantly. Maybe things were tidying up pretty nicely for Amelia, but the fight was far from over for me.

Kanzeil was still out there, probably downright manic to get to me now.

***

The cold, foggy night gave way to a gloomy dawn. Heavy clouds hung over Saillune City and stifled the usual gleam of the Royal Palace. If I didn't know better, I'd say the collective moods of Gourry, Clawfell, Phil, and I—after we'd brought Phil up to speed on the events of the evening—had something to do with the nasty weather that morning.

Alfred had offered no resistance when we'd hauled him in—the benefit of capturing somebody who's knocked out cold. He was put under lock and key in a compound not far from the palace grounds. But while Alfred posed no immediate threat, his father still did. Christopher knowing about the assassination plots, or even working as an accomplice, were definite possibilities. So, our next step was to find out how involved Christopher really was in his son's conspiracy.

Gourry and I tagged along when Phil went looking for Christopher around the palace, and the three of us finally found the man sitting alone, pensively, in the lobby of the main hall.

I got the feeling Christopher had already heard about Alfred's arrest. Streaks of silver now glinted in his dark hair and his shoulders hunched in uncharacteristic defeat.

"Chris?" Phil asked calmly.

Christopher slowly looked up, gazing at us with bloodshot eyes. He made a sound in his throat like a stifled laugh; then, with a self-mocking leer on his lips, he muttered, "What sort of brother am I?"

Phil exhaled deeply. "So you're already aware of what's happened." He drew up a chair across from Christopher and took a seat. Gourry and I stood on either side of Phil, ready to draw our swords if Christopher tried anything funny.

Christopher nodded weakly, a wan, ironic smile crossing his lips. "What's become of him?" Christopher asked. "Al, I mean."

"He's still unconscious, but he should be coming around soon." Christopher sighed deeply and buried his face in his hands. "I'll admit it," he moaned after a moment. "This is all my fault."

That caught Phil off guard. He locked his eyes on Christopher, his brows laced.

"I'm the one who filled his head with these ambitions," Christopher explained. "Now that I think of it . . . whenever he came to me for advice, all I did was complain to him about my *own* circumstances." He sunk in his seat and shook his head despairingly. "I've always been jealous. And I ranted to him all the time about how, if I'd been born first, it would be me instead of you as heir to the throne."

I sensed confusion and anger simmering from Phil. He was obviously trying to keep a lid on it as he momentarily shifted his gaze over to me and then to Gourry. Christopher, however, was oblivious.

"How much happier we'd all be right now," he said, "if I had stopped him when he introduced me to Kanzeil and began speaking openly about his plot to seize the throne.

There was a part of me that wanted him to succeed, and yet each day I hated what my son was intending to do more and more. It seems that, though I never admitted it to myself, entangling my son with my own ambitions was the cause of this whole disaster."

Christopher fixed his reddened eyes on his brother. "If nothing else," he said in a cracked voice, "as a father, that's what I regret most of all." He sighed again, slumped in his chair, and let a single manly tear roll down his cheek.

Sniffling, Christopher continued, "I care not how I'm judged. My ambitions nearly ruined us all—they began with me and they shall end with me. However . . . please have mercy on my son. Understand that he was merely a victim, blinded by his foolish father's vain ambitions." He glanced sympathetically at Gourry and me, "I know it depends on the severity of his crimes, but please do not punish him too harshly."

Phil clasped his hands and perched at the edge of his chair. "That," he said thoughtfully, "depends on Alfred."

At that moment, a sudden clamoring emerged from the guards outside. The doors burst open and a figure appeared in the doorway, silhouetted by daylight.

There was no mistaking that frantically pawed hair. Alfred.

What, already back for more?!

Alfred stood with squared shoulders and panted heavily. He lowered the drawn blade in his hand.

Christopher jumped out of his seat. "Al?!"

A small stampede of guards rushed through the doors, swords and spears in hand. They kept their distance from Alfred, though, the way you do from a mad dog in the street.

"Stay back!" Alfred roared at them. He turned his glare in our direction and began skulking toward us.

"Al?!" Christopher repeated, his voice a few pitches higher. "What have you—?"

"I broke out, Father! What did you think? That I was going to stay locked up in that doghouse forever?!"

In his typically quiet tone, Phil asked, "And what about the guards?"

Alfred broke out in a fit of laughter. "Guards?!" he threw back. He shook his head, a frenzied smile on his lips.

"Don't make me laugh! You think a couple of your pathetic guards are going to keep me put? You've got some real arrogant soldiers working for you, I'll give you that. Want to know what they said to me?"

Alfred struck a prissy pose, and in a babyish sing-song cooed: "We can't wet you weave here. Now get in your wittle woom and stay quiet!" He cackled like a maniac, and I think everyone in the room got just a *little* more uncomfortable.

Alfred halted a few feet away from us and stared admiringly at his sword. "I let them know what I thought of their attitudes," he drawled. "And I'm sure they're regretting it right now . . . in Hell!"

"Al!" Christopher interrupted. "That's enough!"

Nice work, Dad. What next? You gonna ground him for a week?

The guards stood poised at the doorway, ready to make a move against Alfred. But, like Gourry and me, they were unsure of what to do. It had suddenly become quite a hothouse in there. For the time being, all any of us could do was stand our ground and wait for something to happen.

"Stop," Christopher pleaded, his voice shaking. "Please, no more, Alfred. It's over."

Alfred's eyes blazed and he shook his head furiously. "No, it isn't! You're wrong, Father! It's not over yet! It's not over at all!"

He drew closer to Phil. That maddened look in his eyes officially worried me—and Gourry too, apparently, because we both drew our swords just as Phil rose to his feet.

"No!" Christopher cried. He suddenly jumped forward, stepping between Phil and Alfred. "Stop this, Alfred!"

Alfred gnashed his teeth in frustration so loudly I could hear it from where I was standing. "Father!" he snarled. "Step aside!"

"I won't," Christopher shot back emphatically. "Stop this madness right now!"

"Out of my way!" Alfred lunged past his father toward Phil.

"Alfred!"

SMACK!

The two of them collided. Christopher, in a flash, grabbed Alfred's shoulder with one hand. Then a thin trickle of blood leaked out of the corner of his mouth.

Alfred crumpled to the floor. His tongue flitted from side to side, and his mouth made trembling movements like he was trying to say something. It was when my eyes fixed on Alfred's chest that I realized what had happened: Christopher had run his self-defense dagger straight into Alfred's heart. A thick red stain slowly spread across his shirt.

"It . . . ends here," Christopher grunted. A sad, resigned smile came over his face. "I've been a failure . . . of a father . . ."

And as if that bit of drama hadn't been enough, Christopher then turned the dagger around on himself. He was about to thrust the blade into his own belly when Phil jumped in and stopped him.

"Brother!" Christopher wailed, tears spilling down his cheeks. "Why won't you let me die?!"

"Because," Phil replied, prying the dagger out of Christopher's hands. "Because you're my brother."

Phil flung the dagger and stared with pitying eyes as the broken, shuddering Christopher slowly sank to his knees. Phil paused a moment, then carefully knelt down and wrapped his arms around his brother.

It was a touching scene, I have to admit. Gourry cried. I was fine, though.

. . . *Sniff.*

***

"Heading out already?"

That chirrupy voice could only belong to one person, particularly that early in the morning.

"Yeah, Amelia," I continued to pack up my things as she skipped into my bedroom. "There's still some business

I've gotta take care of. It's . . . well . . . kinda pressing." My business was, in fact, a face-to-face with Kanzeil, but I wasn't about to tell her that.

I didn't much savor the idea of leaving the comforts of the palace now that all the noise had died down. And my idea of a much-deserved rest certainly didn't include squaring off with a teleportation-happy Mazoku. But sounding worried around Amelia would've just gotten the girl all worked up.

"Mm-hmm." Amelia didn't sound too convinced. In fact, she glanced at me a little dubiously and sported a small frown. "Are you keeping something from me, Miss Lina?"

Keeping something? Where'd you get that idea?

"N-no," I blurted. Just to drive my point home, I waved a dismissing hand at her.

"Not me," I continued, chuckling this time. "You don't have to worry. I'm not about to run off with the palace silverware."

Wow, that wasn't funny. Especially since I'd stashed a very nice spoon in my cloak pocket.

"That's not what I meant!" Amelia complained. "There's something else, isn't there?"

"Something else?"

"Yes! Like, wasn't Kanzeil trying to kill you? I bet you're going after him."

I shrugged. "And since when do I go looking for trouble?"

Oops. I think we both knew the answer to that question.

"I knew it!" Amelia snapped her fingers. "You're after Kanzeil! Who is he, anyway? Why is he so bent on killing you?"

"Whatever," I said, still trying to sound nonchalant. "He has his reasons, I guess."

But as to what those reasons were, I honestly had no clue. They definitely had nothing to do with royal rumbling in Saillune, so I didn't feel the need to get into it with Amelia.

"Really?" Amelia asked. "You mean he's got reasons to hold a grudge against you?"

That girl was not gonna get off my back!

"That's what I said," I replied shortly. "Reasons. But what're you so curious about, anyway?" I figured if she was going to poke into my business, I could poke right back.

"Because," she proclaimed with a raised fist, "justice burns in my blood."

Uh, okay. Good luck with that.

"See, lately, I've sensed all sorts of things kicking up . . . like dust in a storm." She began to pace, her forehead slightly wrinkled in sage contemplation. "I've sensed it in places I can see and places I can't. I feel like something *big* has been set into motion. Call it a feeling about the Fate of the World," she parted the air with her hands, "but my Justice Sense tells me that evil is afoot."

What the hell is Justice Sense? I'll have to pick some up on my way out.

I was willing to concede that whatever Amelia could feel was tied to her priestess powers, but calling it Justice was just tacky.

"Lina," she continued, "I know from the bottom of my heart that you're a good person. And yet I don't know why or how, but I get the sense that you're bound to whatever evil is stirring up out there."

Amelia had put me in a tight spot. She was right, of course—evil was at work somewhere out there, and it was going to involve me. But I wasn't about to admit that her intuition was on the money, and get her tagging along with us on our quest for Kanzeil. *That* was an absolute no-no. So, I tried to downplay it.

"You're thinking about it too much," I told her with a flippant smirk.

Smooth, Lina. Very smooth.

***

Knock knock.

I knew that double tap. "Come on in," I called from the edge of my bed. I glanced up from staring at my feet to see Gourry poke his head into the room; his smile as vacant as ever.

"Yo!" he said.

Gourry and I had checked into a small inn in the bustling heart of Saillune City. Sure, we could've blown out of the city after leaving the Royal Palace that morning, but the streets were a lot livelier now that the dust and smoke of political danger had settled. We'd treated ourselves to a day of sightseeing and one fabulous and monster-free supper.

"Something on your mind, Gourry?" I asked him.

"I dunno," he replied vaguely, sinking into a big chair beside the nightstand.

Gourry sounded spaced-out. I wasn't much in the mood for small talk, so I just went back to staring at the floor. I must've been awfully quiet, because Gourry—who's usually clueless about these things—eventually asked if I was all right.

"I'm fine," I replied. "Why?"

"C'mon." Gourry frowned. "You swung from bubbly to broody and back again all day today. And at supper, you were real quiet; you usually chat up a storm while you're piggin' out."

"So, out with it," Gourry said. "What's bothering you?"

"Mmm . . ." I wasn't sure how to put it.

"Look," added Gourry, sitting up in his chair. "I know I'm not the smartest lantern in the tool shed, but you can at least trust me. And even if I can't help you, talking about whatever it is might make you feel better."

From the tavern downstairs came the rowdy chorus of men's voices, all drunk and ignorantly happy. I sighed.

"Well," I said at last, "I guess I can't keep it from you forever." I caught his eyes. "This morning, Amelia said she felt a powerful evil stirring, Gourry. An evil *I'm* connected to."

"That's a pretty harsh thing to say."

"Y'think?" I sighed again. "Anyway, that's why I've been so down in the dumps."

Gourry chewed on the edge of his forefinger. "So," he said after a moment. "Do you always think about deep stuff like this?"

"Deep stuff? My life's on the line here, Gourry! And I need to know why Kanzeil wants to kill me!"

"Whoa, whoa!" Gourry threw out his hands. "What does Kanzeil have to do with powerful evil?"

This is gonna be a long night.

Luckily, Gourry was willing to try and catch up. He thought deeply for a few minutes, and I could've sworn I smelt burning rubber.

"Kanzeil," he muttered at last. "You never met him before Saillune, right? That means he couldn't be after you for, like, getting a fist in the mouth during one of your legendary bar fights." He drummed his fingers on the chair's armrest.

"Wait a sec!" Gourry suddenly jumped up like his butt had hit a tack. "He mentioned Seigram and how he sucks once, didn't he? Maybe Seigram went crying back to Kanzeil after we beat him up!"

I couldn't help but smile at the thought of Seigram bawling like a baby after we'd given him a thrashing. "Cute," I replied. "But, I don't think so."

"Damn." Gourry flopped back in his chair. "That was my best guess. Why do *you* think he's after you, Lina?"

"Honestly," I told him, "I have no idea."

That's when it hit me. Maybe Kanzeil *didn't* have anything against me—nothing personal, anyway. Maybe he was after me at the behest of the entire Mazoku race.

When I told Gourry my theory, he looked at me with such confusion that I thought he was going cross-eyed. I'd definitely fried his brains with that one.

"That definitely explains it," I commented, biting my lip. In fact, my theory fit the situation perfectly, and it was beginning to freak me out.

The short version goes like this: A little while ago, Gourry and I fought the *very* high-ranking Demon Lord Ruby Eye Shabranigdu. Through a combination of hard work and extreme luck, we'd even taken the guy down. But there was more to it than that—Shabranigdu comes with a social and historical context.

It all began in ancient times, back in the Age of Legends, when Shabranigdu—was sundered into seven pieces. Now, every sorcerer and warrior (except for Gourry) knows that tale. The twist, however, took place about a thousand years ago, when one part of the Demon Lord was revived but sealed in the ice of the Kataart Mountains. From there, it's said he began to preside over all the Mazoku of the world.

Kanzeil potentially pursuing me at the orders of the Demon Lord of the North suddenly made a lot of sense. I mean, would you let someone who had destroyed a part of your own flesh and blood get away with it? Of course not. Even Gourry would vow revenge.

"Did you," Gourry began slowly, "do anything recently that could've ticked off the Mazoku?" I read no sarcasm in his tone. The guy was straight-faced and totally serious.

Gourry!

"Hello!" I called to him, reaching over to make a knocking gesture against his forehead. "Don't you remember our little incident with Ruby Eye? The guy I destroyed with a spell even stronger than Dragon Slave?"

Gourry, his eyes screwed in my direction, nodded blankly. "Uhh . . . what about it?"

"Gods!" I cried, slapping my own face. "Don't you get it already?!"

"Nope," he replied serenely. "I sure don't."

I paused. "I apologize," I muttered at last. "I thought you just might have a brain."

"Do I really seem that stupid to you?"

"LISTEN," I snarled, hammering each word like a nail into Gourry's head. "When we defeated Ruby Eye, we proved it was possible for a human to bring down a top-ranking Mazoku. Okay?

"We definitely destroyed that piece of Shabranigdu, but since that battle I've thought plenty about the other piece of the Demon Lord, the one sealed in the Kataart Mountains to the north. The scattered pieces of Shabranigdu are probably separate parts of a single consciousness, with each piece connected to the others regardless of the distance between them. So, when I dispatched Ruby Eye with a spell even more powerful than Dragon Slave, that naturally pissed off the Demon Lord. He must've immediately ordered his demon assaasins to hunt me down, and Kanzeil could easily be one of 'em.

"*That's* what Amelia was talking about," I concluded. "*That* must be the evil she sensed at work in the world."

Gourry's expression was as vapid as ever. Nothing came out of his mouth except for a bit of spit at the corners of his lips.

"*Don't-you-get-it?*" I asked through my teeth, desperately trying to reign in my frustration.

"I-I think so," Gourry driveled. "You mean things are really messed up right now, right?"

"*Really* messed up," I insisted. "If I'm right, even if we destroy Kanzeil, the Demon Lord's only going to send more assassins after me. More and more . . . until one of them kills me." I swallowed, my exasperation with Gourry quickly giving way to the dread of imminent death.

"Whoa," mumbled Gourry. "You're taking this really calm, considering."

"No, I'm *not*, brainiac." I waved a hand. "And there are still things that my theory can't explain."

Gourry gave me a sidelong look. "Like?"

I raised my right forefinger. "For instance," I offered, "why did Kanzeil use the attacks that he did? If he's really trying to kill me, why didn't he let loose with some heavy stuff during that in-city fight? I get the feeling he's holding back, but Mazoku aren't the type to go easy on anyone—leastways humans."

"Maybe he was afraid of messing up the block."

"Yeah, right," I drawled. "Somehow, I don't think a Mazoku give a rat's ass about property damage."

Gourry settled back in his chair. "Hmm . . . whatever it is, it still sounds like you're planning on chasing him down for a final fight."

"Like I have a choice." I shook my head. "If I don't, he'll just come after me again and again 'til my luck runs out. Better I find him than he finds me."

Gourry slapped his knees and stood up. "Well, whatever happens, I'm glad we had this chat. I find talking things through always helps settle the mind, don't you?"

"Anyway," I said, "I'm not sure how much it helped, but thanks for looking in on me."

Gourry blinked. "Are you trying to tell me that nothing I said helped you?"

I had to smile. If anything, Gourry had cheered me up a bit with his nonsense, and that was definitely worth something.

"Hey," I said after a minute, getting to my feet. "How about you and me grab a late-night snack down in the tavern? It'll be my treat."

Gourry raised an eyebrow. "Well, well," he murmured. "That's strangely generous of you."

"Well, the first course is on me." I stretched out my arms and winked. "Then you're on your own."

***

Gourry and I traveled a wide gravel highway that wound its way for miles and miles through the woods and forests before finally reaching the Kingdom of Gairia.

And there, at the side of the road, stood Kanzeil. He waited calmly for us as he leaned against a tree.

"Sorry to keep you waiting," I said evenly.

Kanzeil shrugged. "I've been waiting to kill you for a long time," he answered coldly. "And a few extra days mean very little when you've lived as long as I have."

Even with the distance we'd traveled, we were still close enough to potentially torch Saillune City if we fought where we stood. My first priority was to somehow get us as far away from there as possible.

I shouldn't have worried. Kanzeil began walking away from the city, following the highway.

"This way," he ordered. "I know a more suitable place for combat."

Gourry and I glanced at each other. Kanzeil seemed like a smart guy—I'm sure he knew that if he challenged me in the middle of the city, I'd have to fight with my kiddie gloves.

Unless he planned to fight in a *different* city? That, of course, led me to a pressing question.

"Kanzeil," I asked after we'd tramped along for several minutes, "where are we going?"

"We cannot fight so close to the city," he murmured. "We would risk harming or killing other humans."

Okay—*that* threw me. Gourry and I went bug-eyed with puzzlement.

"Th-that's very humane of you," I stuttered at last.

"Don't misunderstand," Kanzeil replied hastily. "Nothing would please me more than to raze the entire city of Saillune. But I've been ordered not to harm any human beings—other than you, of course, and any human assassins I've hired as help. I'm merely following orders."

Ah ha! So that was why, when we'd faced off against Kanzeil in the city, he'd disappeared as soon as we'd started using Alfred's men as shields. Then again, if Kanzeil was forbidden to harm humans, why was Zuuma exempt from that order?

If you think getting inside Gourry's head is difficult, try a Mazoku–it's damn near impossible.

"Whose orders?" I asked.

Kanzeil turned around suddenly, pointing at Gourry. "You, human—Gourry, is it? I will not destroy you. You will still be alive, hence I cannot reveal my master's name."

Fine. Be that way, ya big meanie!

That got me nowhere. Quickly, I switched angles with a different question. "Okay, so then why are you after me?"

"You're in the way," Kanzeil replied flatly.

"Of course I am," I pressed. "But *why* am I in the way? If we're gonna fight to the death, then I think I at least deserve the courtesy of knowing why I was challenged in the first place."

"And I'd like to tell you. But it just so happens that I don't know the reason, either."

I tried to edge a bit of disdain into my voice. "So, you're just an errand boy, is that it?"

"That is correct," Kanzeil answered, apparently unperturbed.

So, the guy was composed and orderly in addition to being evil and murderous.

"Since we haven't gotten to our battleground yet," I went on, "I'd like to ask you a few other things. Whatever happened to Zuuma? Last time I saw him, he was short one arm and barbequing the other."

"I don't know," Kanzeil replied. "After that fight, he vanished. I know nothing more."

"By my last count, you made, let's see . . . three attempts on me at the Royal Palace. Am I right?"

"Correct. And they failed for the same reason I couldn't fight you properly in the city." In other words, loads of pesky humans around.

As he spoke, Kanzeil turned at a fork in the road and onto a narrow path leading deeper into the forest. I got the feeling our stage was nearing.

While I had Kanzeil talking, I thought I'd try another question. "Where'd you get those weird, creepy monsters for attempt number two and the nasty beetle for attempt number three?"

"Those monsters you're referring to," he answered, "were low-ranking demons. When they manifest themselves in this world, they cannot continue to exist on their own power unless they possess an inhabitant of *this* realm or transmogrify. Their form in their natural realm is quite distinct; I don't know how they appeared in your eyes."

Whoa. I'd always wondered about lesser demons. That also explained why physical attacks hadn't worked against our lunch.

It was real gracious of Kanzeil to let me in on all this. I'd have to write everything up if I survived our fight; the Sorcerer's Guild would pay a pretty penny for that kind of report.

"The third attempt," Kanzeil continued, "made use of one of the demon beasts slumbering beneath the magma of Clawveil Volcano. I'm sure you know of its might."

"*One* of them?" I asked, unable to mask my stunned surprise. "How many are there?"

"Even I don't know that."

"Any other questions?" Kanzeil asked flatly.

I thought about that for a second.

"I've got one more for you, Kanzeil. It sounds a bit far-fetched, but you didn't, by any chance, have anything to do with that little brouhaha back in Saillune, did you? What I mean is, did you put Alfred under your spell and make him do those crazy things?"

"You're reading too much into it," he snapped. "Alfred was looking for a strongman to put his plan into action. I merely arranged for him to find me."

"I see," I said. "All right, that clears that."

"Good."

We continued our steady tread on the narrow path. After a few more minutes, the forest opened onto a surprisingly wide, grassy plain the whole of Saillune City could've fit into.

Convenient.

The path cut the plain before continuing through the forest on the other side. It was a weird place for a giant meadow—like mammoth hands had cleared a space in the center of the forest as some sort of afterthought—but it was definitely spacious and secluded. It seemed as if all the birds and animals had fled the area before we'd even gotten there, probably sensing the imminent battle and wanting to clear out beforehand. I didn't blame them.

Kanzeil stopped at the entry to the meadow and turned to us. "We have arrived at our destination," he announced. "The gentleman must now depart and leave us to our business."

I definitely didn't want Gourry to go. "Oh, c'mon," I drawled as convincingly as I could. "Just let him stay. You could beat us *both* with your hands tied behind your back, right?" Rule Number One for getting an opponent to lose the advantage: stroke his ego.

Kanzeil glared at me with his snakelike eyes, then flicked them over to Gourry. "As you wish," he replied after a moment. "Shall we begin?"

But we were way ahead of him; Gourry and I had already sprinted off across the meadow. I know that running away from a Mazoku with teleportation powers is pretty meaningless, but I wanted to buy myself time for some spell-chanting.

When I spun around, I was surprised to see that Kanzeil had hardly moved. Was he waiting for me to strike first? *Sounds good to me*, I thought as I chanted my first spell.

"Ragna Blast!"

CHOOM!

A reverse pentagram blazed in the ground around Kanzeil. Its five interior sides tapered upward 'til they met and formed a black pillar that surged downward, ensnaring Kanziel. Black plasma shot from all sides of the pillar, charging the inside with deadly energy levels. The power was intense enough to vaporize a brass demon in a blink.

But not Kanzeil, apparently.

"Ha!" he laughed from within the plasma pillar. "Not bad . . . for a human." His tone was disturbingly nonchalant. "And yet far beneath my kind."

As he spoke, Kanzeil clenched his fists and flung his arms outward, breaking the bonds that held the pillar together. The spell shattered around him like a piece of glass.

"What?!" I cried out, stumbling backward.

Kanzeil raised his arm. A magic light, as thin as a thread, shot from one of his fingertips and made a beeline for me.

"Not today!" Gourry boomed. He threw himself in front of me to deflect the beam with his Sword of Light. But just before it came within reach, the magic beam suddenly zigzagged around Gourry and shot right into my legs.

"OW!"

My knees buckled from the overwhelming jolt of pain and I tumbled onto the grass. Both my thighs and my ankles had been seared; it wasn't heavy damage, and I wasn't bleeding, but it hurt like hell.

It wasn't a bad strategy: immobilize your opponent before going in for the kill. "Lina!" The color in Gourry's face had drained, and he looked absolutely terrified.

"I'm all right!" I shouted. "Minimal damage." I managed a weak—and probably really awkward—smile.

"Just the way I like it," Kanzeil murmured, his words curling into the afternoon air like smoke from a smoldering fire. His voice sounded almost seductive or blissful, like he was getting the foot massage of his life. "I won't finish you off quickly. Whether you die from pain or from madness, just know that your death will not be peaceful either way."

A chill ran up my spine. Kanzeil was *enjoying* this. Unfortunately for me, I didn't find any glee in hearing that my infinitely-more-powerful opponent had just decided to torture me to death.

"What's wrong?" Kanzeil asked. "You seem disappointed." His lips contorted into an icy—strike that, *crazy*—smile.

Disappointed? More like freaked beyond belief, but he was on the right track. I didn't want to encourage him any more by wincing, so I struggled to my feet with as straight a face as possible. I needed to act, and *fast*. I probably only had one shot, so I figured I'd put some flavor into it.

"Back off!" Gourry shouted. "What are you tryin' to do?!"

Uh . . . kill me! Haven't you been listening?!

Kanzeil turned his gaze to Gourry. "Do you not know what Mazoku consume to live?" he asked darkly, his glare unwavering as he slowly walked toward us. "The source of our power is miasma, the *negative* emotions that living things produce. Fear, anger, sadness, despair . . . to my kind, these are supreme delicacies. The agony of torture is simply the most effective method to bring them forth."

My blood ran cold. I suddenly realized why Kanzeil looked and sounded almost hungry, and why that hadn't come out until now. He had all the time in the world in this field—no random humans to dodge, no other conspiracies to play along with. He was planning on a nice, slow feeding, and whatever anguish he could draw from Gourry and me was the main freakin' course.

Just get a goddamn sandwich and leave us alone!

The good news was that during Kanzeil's cryptic little lecture, I'd chanted my next spell.

"Dragon Slave!"

"What?!" Kanzeil halted in his tracks. "Dammit!"

KABOOOM!

A brilliant red light engulfed the Mazoku, who only had the chance to sneer before a tremendous explosion went off with him inside it. The shockwave hit Gourry and me with considerable force. I painfully dug my heels into the ground and threw my arm up over my face, squinting against the blast to watch the resulting incineration.

Dragon Slave is considered the most powerful spell a human can cast. Since it draws its power from the overlord of all darkness and Ruby Eye Shabranigdu, even a powerful Mazoku lacks the strength to resist it.

"Got him!" Gourry cried exultantly.

I cringed from the pain that coursed through my legs, but still managed to give Gourry a quick wink of acknowledgment.

"Hmph," came a voice, "got me indeed."

I jerked my head up. A lone dark figure emerged from the dispersing veil of smoke. As it got closer, I realized that the spell did have a pretty nasty effect on Kanzeil, but definitely not the kind of effect I'd been expecting.

Kanzeil no longer had any hair, just a few singed wisps here and there on his bare head. He had no ears, no nose, no mouth, and the skin on his face looked as blue as a frozen corpse's. Weirdest, though, were his eyes—they were lidless and way bigger than any human's.

Ew!

It was Kanzeil as he really was; his true form on the earthly plane. But blue-faced or not, how was he still walking when I'd hit him with Dragon Slave?

"It seems that you underestimated the Demon Race. Even a spell that draws its power from Shabranigdu must still be channeled through a *human*. Such a spell may be sufficient in neutralizing a low-ranking demon, but against a mid-ranking demon such as myself, it's hardly enough to wipe me out with a single blow."

"M-mid-ranking?!" I blurted.

"Is this the first time you've seen a real Mazoku's power?" Kanzeil's giant eyes narrowed. "Or did you not consider that the Mazoku you've thus far confronted have been of the lowest order?"

He slowly drew closer to me as he spoke.

"Stay back!" Gourry shouted, holding his Sword of Light aloft. He stepped in front of me and whipped the blade hard in Kanzeil's direction.

"Out of my way!" Kanzeil roared. He raised his left hand skyward, unleashing a shockwave. Gourry parried the shockwave with his magic blade, but since it was stronger than he'd prepared for, the wave forced him backward and out of the way.

Now there was nothing between Kanzeil and me.

A strange rasping chortle came from Kanzeil. His giant eyes relaxed, and he seemed to almost smile, if smiling without a mouth is possible. He raised his forefinger and pointed straight at me.

The magic beam shot out again, skewering me in my side! My voice clenched in my throat as I collapsed to the ground, coiled up against the pain.

"Stop it!" Gourry cried, running furiously toward Kanzeil with his Sword of Light blazing.

Kanzeil was following through on his promise: by missing all my vital organs, he was on his way to torturing me to death. The pain searing in my side spun my senses and blurred my eyes. Kanzeil halted his assault for a moment, just long enough for me to regain my senses and, assumedly, get hurt again.

He shot another beam, this time into my other side. I gasped and arched my back as a silent scream exploded in my head.

Gourry shouted something and took a wicked swing with his sword. But in the instant before the sword hit its mark, a blackness swallowed up Kanzeil, shielding him and repelling Gourry's attack.

"Stop it, stop it, STOP IT!" Gourry cried.

Kanzeil laughed gleefully as Gourry hacked away with his sword.

"Yes," Kanzeil exclaimed. "Yes! I can feel your anger, your despair! How delicious you are."

I must've blacked out for a moment because when I next gained consciousness, I found myself cradled in Gourry's arms.

I don't know how he did it. Not only had Gourry managed to shield me from further attacks, but he had moved me out of Kanzeil's reach.

"Lina!" Gourry pleaded. "Hang in there! Lina!"

"G-Gourry . . ." I breathed, struggling to get my bearings back. I could barely move and my eyes were blurred with tears, but I was aware of one thing: I wasn't going to die.

Gourry pushed his lips to my ear. "Listen to me," he whispered hoarsely. "Lina, you've gotta use *it*."

"It?" I mumbled vaguely.

"Use *that* spell," Gourry insisted. "The strongest you've got! You hear me? Use it!"

That spell? My mind snapped to attention. Giga Slave was the most powerful spell I knew, and I was possibly the only one who could cast it. It drew on the power of a Mazoku even greater than Ruby Eye: The Lord of Nightmares. In fact, I'd used Giga Slave to defeat Shabranigdu.

It was a far more powerful spell than Dragon Slave, and even Kanzeil, that cocky bastard, was unlikely to survive it. There was one drawback, though. A major one.

Me.

"I can't," I whispered to Gourry.

"Why not?!"

"I can't control the spell while injured like this. And if I can't control it, it's too great a risk. I might kill *everyone*."

When I said I could kill everyone, I meant *everyone*. Not just me, Gourry, Kanzeil, and the inhabitants of Saillune City. I meant *everyone on Earth*.

And since Giga Slave absorbs a massive amount of life-force energy from its wielder, I knew I could get killed just trying the damn thing. I pondered this for a moment.

"You got any other options?!" Gourry asked feverishly.

"There is," I sputtered, "but—"

"No buts!" he exclaimed. "Just do it!"

Well, Gourry had asked for it, and now there was no turning back.

"What do you want me to do?" he whispered.

"First thing, keep him off me. Keep at him with your sword like you were doing before. Use everything you've got!"

Gourry nodded. "What else?"

"Leave the rest to me."

Gourry nodded again. "Gotcha!" he said, rising to his feet and regripping his sword.

Kanzeil, hairless, faceless, but still in the game, watched as Gourry turned to him.

"Coming back for more?" He still wore that jubilant expression on his non-face, his eyes absolutely twinkling with glee.

Kanzeil jutted his palm out, emitting a flash of light that knocked Gourry off his feet and sent him tumbling through the grass.

Meanwhile, I gritted my teeth and managed to get to my feet.

"Oh ho," Kanzeil twittered cheerfully. There was even a hint of admiration in his voice. "Look at you."

I tried to ignore his blather and instead focused on chanting Dragon Slave, but with a new spin.

Thou who art darker than night . . .

Kanzeil's face contorted into an ugly display of scorn. His eyes bore into me with disdain, as if I were some doddering idiot not worth his time.

"Is that Shabranigdu's incantation again?" he spat. "Please, don't waste your breath."

Gourry, in the meantime, had stumbled back to his feet. He took a deep breath, readying his sword.

. . . *Thou who art redder than the flowing blood* . . .

"How pathetic," Kanzeil growled. "Your final stand and that's the best you can do? I'm sorely disappointed. I took you for someone a bit more . . . imaginative."

. . . *Thou through whom time flows* . . .

I could hear Gourry call to me. "I can't take more than one or two more hits, Lina!"

That's when Gourry began tearing through the grass toward Kanzeil. He drew his sword all the way back, ready to deliver his first blow, charging like a rolling thundercloud. I've gotta hand it to Gourry—when things get nasty, he pulls out all the stops.

. . . *I call upon thy exalted name* . . .

Gourry slashed his sword upward, slicing at the column of darkness that enshrouded Kanzeil.

. . . *I pledge myself to darkness* . . .

The Sword of Light smashed against the pillar and was instantly repelled. Gourry grunted as he staggered backward, but then just snarled a cry and charged again.

"You are a pest and a bore," Kanzeil snapped. "I've had enough fun."

. . . Let those fools . . .

Light flared from the hand Kanzeil held high. There was no way Gourry could survive another attack from that distance—but I wasn't ready, I couldn't help him!

Gourry!

"AAAAGH!" Kanzeil shrieked as a blue flame suddenly engulfed him.

Ra Tilt?!

Kanzeil whipped around in the direction of the attack. I saw, not far beyond where Kanzeil stood, a silhouette against the trees.

Amelia!

I had no idea how she'd found us, but that didn't matter—she'd bought me the time I'd needed to finish casting my spell. All that remained were Chaos Words.

Gourry swung the Sword of Light one last time. That was all I needed.

"Dragon Slave!"

Kanzeil, for all the agony he was in, still wouldn't drop the attitude. "Don't waste your time!" he cried. "I'm more powerful than any of your paltry parlor tricks!"

Then, before those bulbous eyes of his, something happened that I'm sure he *never* expected: the Sword of

Light's whitish blade was set ablaze with a furious crimson radiance.

"Whaaat?!" he roared.

Gourry brought down the Sword of Light, slicing Kanzeil in half from top to bottom. Before he even hit the ground, Amelia unleashed another Ra Tilt just to finish the foul thing off. The flames immediately consumed what was left of Kanzeil, turning the Mazoku into white ashen powder. The winds that had been circling the meadow throughout the battle quickly scattered the powder to the skies.

The wind settled, and we all looked at each other. I gazed up as tiny specks of Mazoku sprinkled from the clearing sky . . .

I didn't even feel myself hit the ground.

★★★

"Hey, Lina!"

Not now, Gourry.

"Lina!"

Let me sleep.

"LINA!"

"WHAT?!" I snapped, abruptly rolling over in bed.

Gourry, who was on the cot across from mine, immediately shrunk back. "What'd I say?" he murmured sadly.

I sighed and dropped back on my pillow.

We'd only just defeated Kanzeil the day before, and someone had dragged me to Saillune's mystic infirmary and treated with White Magic spells.

Somebody wake me up in three weeks.

"Sheet changes in fifteen minutes, Miss Inverse," Mr. Gray chirped far too cheerily as he passed through. "Up, up, up! You can sleep after we're done."

I groaned. Lucky for us, Mr. Gray was the head physician at the infirmary. It seemed that our adventure in Saillune had given his business quite a boost—beaten-up guards and soldiers, mainly—so he was busy, happy, and sickeningly efficient. I wanted nothing more than to crawl into a hole and recuperate in peace.

Oh, and he'd told me that Sylphiel was still suffering occasionally from nightmares, but would eventually recover, just like Saillune itself.

I sighed and looked up at Gourry, my eyelids still half-closed. "Whaddaya want?" I croaked. It was the first sentence I'd uttered since the battle.

Gourry fiddled with the fringe on his pillowcase. "I just . . . y'know, wanted to know how you did it."

"Did what? Beat Kanzeil?"

"Yeah. What'd you do with Dragon Slave?" Gourry asked.

I rubbed my eyes with the back of a hand. "I just directed Dragon Slave into the Sword of Light. The spell converged with the blade, amplifying the spell's power enough to destroy Kanzeil's defenses."

Gourry smiled. "Nice, Lina!"

But then the smile dropped from his face and he froze as if he'd just realized something horrible.

"What a sec," he muttered.

"Yeah?"

"Weren't you worried that the Sword of Light might, you know, blow up or something when it converged with Dragon Slave?"

"W-well," I stammered, "that's, uh . . . ah ha ha!" I smiled as sweetly as I could, hoping Gourry might be won over by how adorable I could be. But he wasn't having any of it.

"Don't gimme that dopey smile! You knew there was chance of that sword exploding and me exploding with it, didn't you? But you went through with it anyway!"

"Hey!" I yelled back. "Didn't you tell me to 'just do it' no matter what the consequences were? I was just following your advice! And there was good reason to take the risk. Remember, Gourry, your sword once absorbed the power of Giga Slave. The chances of it breaking under Dragon Slave were pretty low."

Gourry frowned, unconvinced. "And what do you suppose the risk was?"

"Oh," I answered vaguely, fishing for a number, "I'd say fifty-fifty."

"Whaaat?!" Gourry exclaimed.

"Just *kidding*, Mr. Jumpy. The risk was closer to 10 percent, probably even less."

The danger had passed. Even though the risk *had* been small, I figured the least I could do was level with Gourry now. Unfortunately, the truth didn't make him feel any better.

I knew that The Sword of Light was more powerful than any human who might wield it, but I still wasn't completely sure of its powers . . . hence my constant plot to swipe the sword from Gourry long enough to take up research on it. And keep it, if at all possible.

"I'd like to know something!" It was Amelia. She'd been standing in the doorway, listening in on us. "How did this stuff between you and Kanzeil start, anyway?"

"He was just following orders," I replied. "Seems the puppet master is still at large."

I was now certain that whoever was behind Kanzeil wasn't the Demon Lord of the North or Ruby Eye Shabranigdu. I'd come to that conclusion after reflecting on my conversation with Kanzeil. He'd never referred to Shabranigdu by an official title or with any honorific. Mazoku are very strict about their code, so Kanzeil's slip-of-the-tongue had been a clue to something else, or rather, *someone* else.

"In any case," I commented, "you really saved our butts the other day, Amelia. I wanna thank you for helping us out. But why did you happen to follow us into battle, anyway?"

"There's an easy enough answer to that." Amelia smiled. "I convinced Father to let me out of the Royal Palace, asked around to find out where you were headed, and traced your steps straight out of the city's gates. When I noticed magic spells going berserk in that field off the main highway, I just followed the lights and noise and found you guys."

"Er, no," I muttered. "Not how, *why*. Why were you so concerned about what happened to us?"

"I told you already." She stepped into the room from the doorway. "Remember when I told you something big was going on?"

"Yeah. You said I was mixed up in it."

"That's right. Now, I don't know what that something is, but if it's something evil, I wanna be there to smash it with . . ." Amelia clenched her fist and raised it high in the air. "With my Iron Maul of Justice!"

Gourry and I looked at each other skeptically, but the young priestess was too fired up to notice.

"So, I'll be tagging along on your travels, if you don't mind," Amelia declared. It'll be wonderful working with you.

I stared at her, still unsure whether or not to take her seriously.

"The pleasure is mine?" I said shakily. "But Phil's gonna flip when he finds out—"

"I told you," Amelia said emphatically. "I convinced him to let me leave the palace and do my own thing."

Youdidwhatnow?

Was Phil such a pushover? I doubted Amelia had convinced him so much as *nagged* the hell out of him 'til he gave in.

"It's not fun and games out there, Amelia." I furrowed my eyebrows. "Gourry and I lead dangerous lives. One slip could cost you your life."

"I'm aware of that, thank you very much," she retorted. "But where I come from, it's proper for daughters to journey forth in their youth, enduring life's myriad hardships while charged with a sense of justice. I'd so much prefer that to living cooped up in some Royal Palace all my life. I wanna know what it feels like to really live!"

Gourry still looked shell-shocked by Amelia's proposition. He turned to me. "Um . . . I don't think we can talk her out of this."

I gripped my temples. I could definitely feel a headache coming on.

"Well," she said cheerfully, "now that that's settled, Miss Lina where will we be heading next?"

But now that she mentioned it, I hadn't really given our next step much thought. I'd spent the past day either unconscious or trying to get my head together. If it weren't for the fact that a host of Mazoku (minus Kanzeil, thankfully) were lurking out there and just waiting to kill me, I'd have gone home to pay my folks a nice long visit. But there were more immediate matters to sort out.

I had to find out why all the Mazoku were suddenly after me.

"The Kingdom of Dilse, Amelia," I told her, "the land where dark legends slumber."

AFTERWORD

Author's Official Spokeswoman "**L**"

L: Hi, everyone! It's been awhile! Official Spokeswoman
  "**L**" here!"

A: Uh, Spokeswoman? I'm here too, right behind you. The
  author. Remember me?

L: Whaaaat?! What're *you* doing here?!

A: What am *I* doing here? I just got back from taking a walk.
  And . . . *you* were the one who tried to drop a flowerpot on
  my head as I left the house!

L: Hey, don't look at me. I know a lot of people who'd like
  to drop a flowerpot on your head! Ha ha ha!

A: What did you say?

L: I was just saying I'm glad you're all right.

A: Didn't sound like it.

L: Oh, who cares? You're all right, aren't you? Anyway, I just wanted to say sorry to everyone for the long delay in getting out *Slayers Vol. 4.*

A: Yeah, what took you so long?

L: You're the author! Why don't you ask yourself?!

A: Oh! Uh . . . got me there. A lot of stuff suddenly came up. Can't go into details.

L: Like hell. You could've at least answered fan mail and kept your readers happy while you frittered your time away.

A: Hey, gimme a break, would you? I sent out New Year's cards, didn't I? Of course, I had someone buy them in bulk, and I didn't actually see them . . .

L: Mm-hmm. And here we are with an overdue novel. So?

A: Well . . . at least we got it out. That should count for something, right?

L: Okay, okay, I forgive you.

A: What'd you think of Kanzeil? He was a mean SOB, wasn't he? Strong as hell and no sense of humor. I wouldn't wanna run into *him* in a dark alley.

L: What are you mumbling about? Okay, everyone, it's time for the "L Event Corner."

A: Right, the last one was a drawing contest. It had to do with unseen people. You gonna keep up with that?

L: Until the author croaks.

A: Ha ha! Hey, wait just a . . . whatever, I think your idea of sending people matchbooks as prizes didn't exactly attract a lot of contestants.

L: And whose bright idea was that? They probably thought: "Screw it, this is just some big joke."

A: H-hey, now.

L: What sort of prize might people like? I think illustrations and colored paper could work.

A: That doesn't sound too shabby.

L: I suppose they'd like something *signed*.

A: No waaaay!

L: Hmph. Scrooge! Okay, the name of our current contest—much in-demand by our fans—is called the Totally Clichéd Character Popularity Contest!

A: But isn't that something even doujinshi do? Are we that desperate? Have we completely run out of creative ideas?

L: Goodness, no! I thought of biology or magic-related questions, but then I thought it was way too geeky so I ruled it out. Like asking for a report on Reverse Ohm errors in physical reconstruction.

A: What the heck is that?

L: Nevermind. I just mean that people wouldn't go for it. Anyway, back to the main issue. To avoid confusion— like "**A** is good but **B** is better!" or stuff like that—divide five points among the names of your favorites.

A: You mean assign one point for each of your five characters?

L: Not if you don't want to. You can divide the five points anyway you like. If you have two to four favorites, you can spread the extra points until you get a total of five. That's "**L**-sama's five-point system!"

A: But who's gonna—?

L: Mm? What?

A: Er, I mean the method's fine, but some poor schmuck's gonna have to add all that up.

L: That's okay. You'll be doing it.

A: Whaaaaat?!

L: Not so loud! Anyway, applications must be received at the publisher's head office by the end of '91. Five names will be selected randomly to receive colored paper autographed by the author. But, if we catch someone trying to submit multiple ballots just to pad out their chances of winning the raffle, all identical votes will be buried in the Postcard Cemetery.

A: So, if you'll forgive the time delay, the results of the Totally Clichéd Character Popularity contest will be announced in the Afterword of the next volume. The prizes will be sent to the winners after that.

L: That's fine, but . . . when *is* the next volume?

A: (gulp)

L: You mean you haven't given any thought to it at all? You have no idea what the next volume will be about?

A: N-no, I've been thinking about it. In rough terms, anyway.

L: Rough terms, huh? Well, when our author says "rough," he really means "clueless."

A: No, see, it's about Lina's Giga Slave—

CRUNCH! (sound of something heavy falling)

S: (pant, pant) I did it, **L**-sama! I failed the first time, but I finally knocked out our author using this flowerpot!

L: That's very nice, but we're finished here. The Afterword's already over.

S: Wha?! But I thought I was gonna get to take part!

L: I lied.

S: Noooooooooooo!

L: Well, it's a cruel world. Anyway, see you next time, which, hopefully, won't be too long from now.

(**L** bows. Wooden clappers. Then . . . final curtain.)

IN THE NEXT VOLUME...

Slayers

5

The Silver Beast

Lina has lost her magic and in order for it to be restored, she'll need to travel to Mine—a village where Ruby Eye Shabranigdu is worshiped. When a mysterious priest crosses her path, she agrees to help him get the Clair Bible and the chimera spell in exchange for his protection. Will they be able to get the Clair Bible before it lands in the wrong hands? Or, has the nightmare already begun . . . ?

TOKYOPOP SHOP

A Diva Torn from Chaos
A Savior Doomed to Love

Volume 2
Lumination

Ai continues to search for her place in our world on the streets of Tokyo. Using her talent to support herself, Ai signs a contract with a top record label and begins her rise to stardom. But fame is unpredictable—as her talent blooms, all eyes are on Ai. When scandal surfaces, will she burn out in the spotlight of celebrity?

Preview the manga at:
www.TOKYOPOP.com/princessai

T
TEEN
AGE 13+

BECK: MONGOLIAN CHOP SQUAD

ROCK IN MANGA!

Yukio Tanaka is one boring guy with no hobbies, a weak taste in music and only a small vestige of a personality. But his life is forever changed when he meets Ryusuke Minami, an unpredictable rocker with a cool dog named Beck. Recently returned to Japan from America, Ryusuke inspires Yukio to get into music, and the two begin a journey through the world of rock 'n' roll dreams! With cameos of music's greatest stars—from John Lennon to David Bowie—and homages to supergroups such as Led Zeppelin and Nirvana, anyone who's anyone can make an appearance in *Beck*...even Beck himself! With action, music and gobs of comedy, *Beck* puts the rock in manga!

HAROLD SAKUISHI'S HIGHLY ADDICTIVE MANGA SERIES THAT SPAWNED A HIT ANIME HAS FINALLY REACHED THE STATES!

FOR MORE INFORMATION VISIT: WWW.TOKYOPOP.COM

ARCANA
BY SO-YOUNG LEE

Inez is a young orphan girl with the ability to communicate with living creatures of all kinds. She is the chosen one, and a great destiny awaits her! Inez must bring back the guardian dragon to protect her country's fragile peace from the onslaught of a destructive demon race.

From the creator of TOKYOPOP's *Model* comes an epic fantasy quest filled with wizards, dragons, deception and adventure beyond your wildest imagination.

© SO-YOUNG LEE, DAIWON C.I. Inc.

DEAD END
BY SHOHEI MANABE

When Shirou's memory is suddenly erased and his friends are brutally murdered, he is forced to piece together clues to solve a shocking and spectacular puzzle. As we follow Shirou's journey, paranoia assumes an air of calm rationality and the line between tormenter and prey is often blurred.

© Shohei Manabe

TOKYO MEW MEW A LA MODE
BY MIA IKUMI AND REIKO TOSHIDA

The cats are back, and a new Mew emerges— the first Mew Mew with *two* sets of animal genes. Half cat, half rabbit, Berry joins the Mew Mew team just in time: a new gang is about to appear, and its leader loves wild game like rabbit—well done and served for dinner!

The highly anticipated sequel to *Tokyo Mew Mew* (*Mew Mew Power* as seen on TV)!

© Mia Ikumi and Kodansha